Threaded Together

Threaded Together

• The Pink Ribbon Quilt Project •

CRAFTER'S CHOICE BOOK CLUB
New York

Threaded Together: The Pink Ribbon Quilt Project is a publication of Crafter's Choice Book Club,
1271 Avenue of the Americas, New York, NY 10020

Edited by B. J. Berti

Book design by Monica Elias

All photographs by Richard Lee except for those on pages 7,16, 17, 22, 23, 27, 28, 36, 37, 40, 42, 48, 67, 72, and 96, which are by Maryellen Stadtlander

Directions Editor: Eleanor Levie, Craft Services, LLC
Directions Illustrator: Mario Ferro

All attempts have been made to acknowledge all of the participants in the Pink Ribbon Quilt Project. We would be pleased to hear from anyone who has been left out or if any quilt blocks have been inadvertently misidentified.

A portion of the proceeds from the sale of *Threaded Together: The Pink Ribbon Quilt Project* will be donated to a breast cancer organization.

ISBN: 1-58288-038-7

Printed in the United States of America

CONTENTS

INTRODUCTION BY
B. J. BERTI
7

FOREWORD BY MIMI DIETRICH
9

THE PINK RIBBON QUILTS
11

DIRECTIONS FOR
TWELVE QUILT BLOCKS
95

CONTRIBUTORS AND
ACKNOWLEDGMENTS
129

When we announced the Pink Ribbon Quilt project to the Crafter's Choice Book Club members in the fall of 1999 we had no idea what to expect. Inspired by Mimi Dietrich's *Pink Ribbon Quilts: A Book Because of Breast Cancer,* a Crafter's Choice November 1999 Alternate Selection, we asked our members to create quilt blocks following a Pink Ribbon theme. Based on conversations with others who had done something similar, we had anticipated receiving around 400 blocks from our members—perhaps as many as 800. That seemed quite manageable; we would have enough blocks to assemble into a single quilt, or perhaps two. We would then donate the quilt (or quilts) to an organization to be used to raise funds for breast cancer research or awareness.

Initially the response was in line with what we expected. However, after promoting the project to our members again in early spring of 2000, not hundreds but thousands of quilt blocks poured in from each of the fifty states, parts of Canada, and from countries as distant as Kuwait. In the United States, the majority of quilt squares came from California, New York, Florida, Michigan, and Texas. Quilt groups across the country, such as the Foothills Quilters Guild in Tennessee and the Oak Run Quilters in Florida, rallied to send numerous squares. About a dozen hand-painted quilt squares were submitted by Brownie Troop 70 and Girl Scout Troop 188 in Maryland. By April 15, 2000, the Crafter's Choice Pink Ribbon Quilt project had received an overwhelming response adding up to some 3,500 unique and beautiful blocks.

It was many, many more blocks than we expected or were prepared for. All of us at Crafter's Choice were deeply moved by the response. Many of the submissions were accompanied by poignant tributes explaining the symbols and motifs used in the blocks—deeply personal stories told in scraps of fabric and stitches. For me it was a revelation—to really see, graphically represented by the blocks, how prevalent breast cancer is and how many people it has affected. We found we had to make a rule not to read the heartrending letters when we were opening up the envelopes and removing the quilt blocks.

In the summer of 2000 we took all of the blocks to Quilt Connection—a quilt shop in Berkeley Heights, New Jersey. Ten king-size quilt tops were completed in a weekend marathon of sewing, pinning, pressing, and assembling arranged by Sally Davis and Lois Griffin. Volunteers sewed through the night and by 4 P.M. on Sunday

the tenth Pink Ribbon Quilt top was completed. Leftover blocks were sent to other volunteers to be assembled into quilt tops; all the tops were then sent to other more experienced machine-quilters who, sandwiching batting between the tops and the backings, completed the quilts.

The fact that we have received more than 3,500 blocks speaks to the concern that exists among women about breast cancer, and the desire among Crafter's Choice Book Club members to play a part in conquering the disease. As Mimi Dietrich, a breast cancer survivor, says, "When life gives you a scrap, make a quilt."

— B. J. Berti
Editor in Chief
Crafter's Choice

I was diagnosed with breast cancer in 1994. To celebrate my five-year anniversary as a survivor I wrote *Pink Ribbon Quilts: A Book Because of Breast Cancer*. It is a quilt book, with directions for making quilts, but it also speaks about how quilting carried me through the experience of having breast cancer. It is a book written from my heart, a personal story shared with the quilters of the world. It was a difficult book to write—expressing my feelings and sharing my breast cancer journey, writing about family and friends' reactions, health-care professionals, keeping a positive attitude, and experiences with other survivors. I tried so hard to make the book positive, because I wanted people to know that it is possible to survive this disease. When the book was published, I was very moved by the letters I received from quilters who shared similar experiences, or who had sisters, mothers, grandmothers, daughters, and friends with breast cancer. Quilters wrote to me saying that I touched their hearts and souls. That's when I knew that writing *Pink Ribbon Quilts* was a personal success.

I was especially touched when the Crafter's Choice Book Club chose the book as a selection and asked members to make quilt blocks. What a wonderful legacy! Lives would be celebrated or remembered in a special quilt! I sent a block from one of the Pink Ribbon quilts as a sign of support. I was overwhelmed when Crafter's Choice told me how many blocks they received, and how many quilts they were making. When I went to Houston that year, I went to look at the quilts all by myself—to savor the feelings and messages and support from the quiltmakers—and know that I was not alone.

There is hope in the knowledge that there are many survivors. When you see a pink ribbon, remember that breast cancer awareness increases the survival rate. Remind yourself and others to get mammograms, visit doctors for annual physicals, and perform monthly self-exams. Take care of yourself and hug the people in your life.

It is amazing how many women and men have been touched by this disease. I hope you will be inspired by the many quilters who have shared their voices and expressions in these quilts. They are speaking from their hearts.

I am honored to be writing this foreword.

—Mimi Dietrich

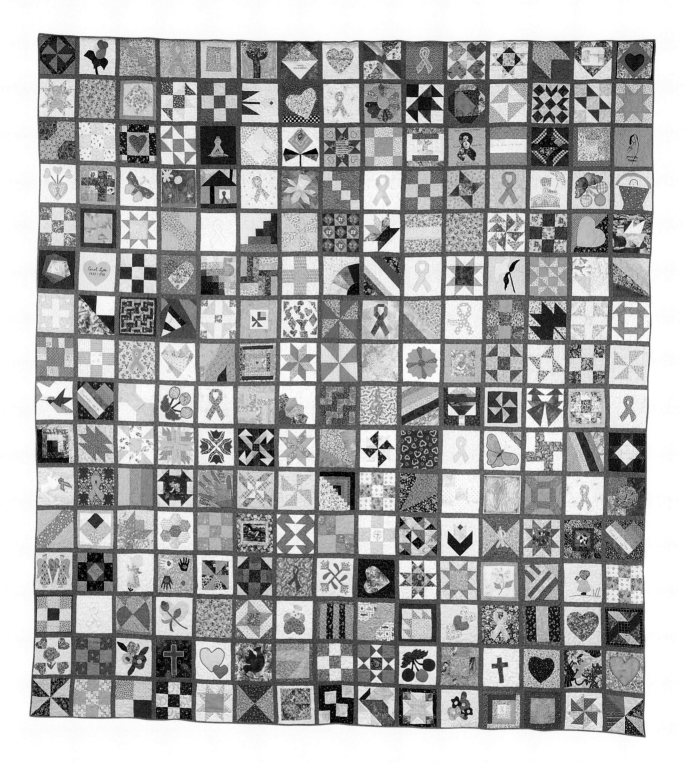

The Pink Ribbon Quilts

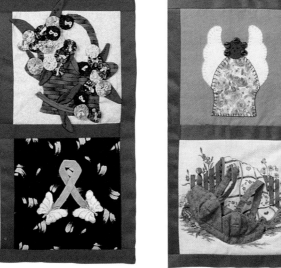

The American quilt has traditionally been an expression of women's hopes, dreams, tragedies, and triumphs. It has been a medium for memorializing the departed and celebrating the milestones of life. As women over the centuries have patched and stitched their personal, family, and community histories into quilts, many have described the act of quilting as a healing pursuit, and a means of working through hard times. Perhaps most important, quilting has always brought women together. All these aspects of quilting tradition and more are embodied in the Pink Ribbon Quilts.

The 3,500 quilt blocks stitched by Crafter's Choice members honor "Vicki D., age 24," "Teresa W., age 38," Elaine C., age 50" and thousands of other individual women who have had breast can-

cer. Stitched together in the Pink Ribbon Quilts by thousands of skilled and loving hands, these personal tributes speak for women everywhere.

Each square tells a story. Some include names, intitials, and ages. Others are embroidered or inscribed with messages, such as "Sew for the Cure." Traditional squares such as Nine Patch, Log Cabin and Cherokee Rose are stitched side by side with original designs, many featuring appliquéd, embroidered, or pieced images—animals, flowers, angels, female figures. Several incorporate photos of beloved mothers, aunts, grandmothers, friends. There is one image of a quilter's father, with the inscription "Men get breast cancer, too."

While the quilts represent overwhelming personal loss, their beauty is exuberant. The Pink Ribbon Quilts embody the fabric of hope, give

expression to grief and remembrance, and stand against isolation. They celebrate our strength and our solidarity.

Before the Civil War, outside of the country's few big cities, women's social lives centered around quilt-making. Early quilters almost always completed their work as a community effort because there was usually only one quilting frame available for an entire region. But what began as a practical necessity came to fill more personal needs. Quilting bees provided a forum not only for serious gossip—something every woman needs—but also for a vital exchange of information in isolated communities. It was while quilting that women shared remedies and recipes and, in general, taught each other what they knew. It sometimes provided an opportunity to pass information from one generation to the next. But perhaps most important, the slow, steady rhythms of sewing together created an atmosphere in which women were able to share their deepest feelings and concerns. In speech and in stitches, the act of quilting brought the personal into the community.

The pattern is called "Cross Roads," which seemed an appropriate pattern to associate with breast cancer— often a crossroads in a woman's life.

—Robin Connors

Community Quilts and Friendship Quilts

While the typical quilting bee was organized to quilt a top that one woman had already pieced on her own, this was not the case with Friendship Quilts. These quilts were a special way for women to show affection for one another, and it seems appropriate to consider The Pink Ribbon Quilts in light of their tradition.

The Friendship Quilt was created as a gift from a community of women to one of their members. Each block was stitched by a different hand. The same pattern was commonly used throughout, but occasionally each block was pieced or appliquéd in a different design. Like so many of the blocks in the Pink Ribbon Quilts, these early friendship blocks often included handwritten or embroidered inscriptions—names, dates, and bits of poetry. When there were as many different designs as there were blocks in the quilt, the final product was known as a Friendship Medley Quilt. Sometimes the quilt was created from start to finish at a party, in a quilting circle filled with warm camaraderie and lively conversation—that snapped to silence if a man entered the room. Each guest brought her favorite scraps and patterns, and stitched up the most stunning and unusual block she could create.

Today, Friendship Quilts, also known as Community Quilts, are often created by people who don't know each other, but have a common bond in their affection for one individual. Typically, one person designs and organizes the project as a gift for a milestone event—a birth, a marriage, a goodbye—or simply to honor someone for long years of friendship or community service. The organizer asks the recipient's friends from far and wide to contribute blocks, sometimes of their own choosing, more often from kits created by the organizer. When the blocks come in, a smaller group gathers to assemble them, and do the quilting.

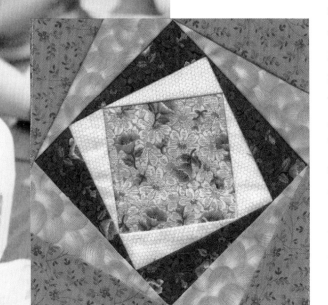

This block is for my mom who died from breast cancer in 1992. With the exception of the muslin back, the fabrics I used are all cut from my mom's blouses, making this block special to me.

—Sherry Rich

The Pink Ribbon Quilts differ from Friendship Medley Quilts and other community quilts in that each block honors a different person, and they were not made as a gift for an individual, but to raise funds and awareness. In this they also have much in common with the sampler album quilts or presentation quilts that became popular in the late-nineteenth century, when quilts with each block created and stitched by a different woman (or occasionally a man) were first created to raise funds for charitable purposes. The most famous of contemporary community quilts, the AIDS Memorial Quilt, also has roots in this tradition.

This block uses two simple patterns. The nine block foundation represents the nine lives I wish for you. The round YoYo's are for laughter's good medicine. Red represents the "war" of your battle. Pink is for "love," for you are wrapped in the Grace of God. The gold stars are your friends and family and the pink beads are their prayers.

—Lucy Koonce

When the AIDS Quilt, organized by the NAMES Project, was first displayed in 1987, it covered a space larger than a football field. Today, it includes more than 44,000 panels, three by six feet in size, each made in honor of a person lost to AIDS. As the epidemic claims more lives, the quilt continues to grow. Widely acclaimed for its role in redefining the tradition of quilt-making in response to the circumstances of our time, it is the largest community art project in the world.

In the spirit of the AIDS Quilt, though on a far smaller scale, each of the Pink Ribbon Quilts, too, is a memorial, a vehicle for fund-raising, a medium for creativity, healing, and education, and a work of art.

As Crafter's Choice Editor in Chief B. J. Berti says in her Introduction, she had a very small project in mind—one or two quilts—when she announced a call for blocks to honor those whose lives have been affected by breast cancer, raise funds for breast cancer research, and increase public awareness of the disease.

The overwhelming response—resulting in fourteen king-size quilts, with blocks to spare—affirms that the Pink Ribbon Quilts represent an international community of women: We all know someone who has had breast cancer; we are all aware of the potential of this disease to impact our own lives and the lives of those we love. When all the individual stories of the project's thousands of pieces are stitched together, one message stands out—this is something we share.

ASSEMBLING THE QUILTS

In the spirit of an old-fashioned quilting party, the task of assembling the first ten quilts over the weekend of June 9-11, 2000, united seventy-five women—most of them strangers to each other—at the Quilt Connection in Berkeley Heights, New Jersey.

"It was phenomenal," recalls Sally Davis, who owns the Quilt Connection, and organized the event with her then-partner Lois Griffin. "The conversation just kept going. No one was ever at a loss for words. It was just like a quilting bee except for the sewing machines. At any given time, we had a minimum of eight to ten

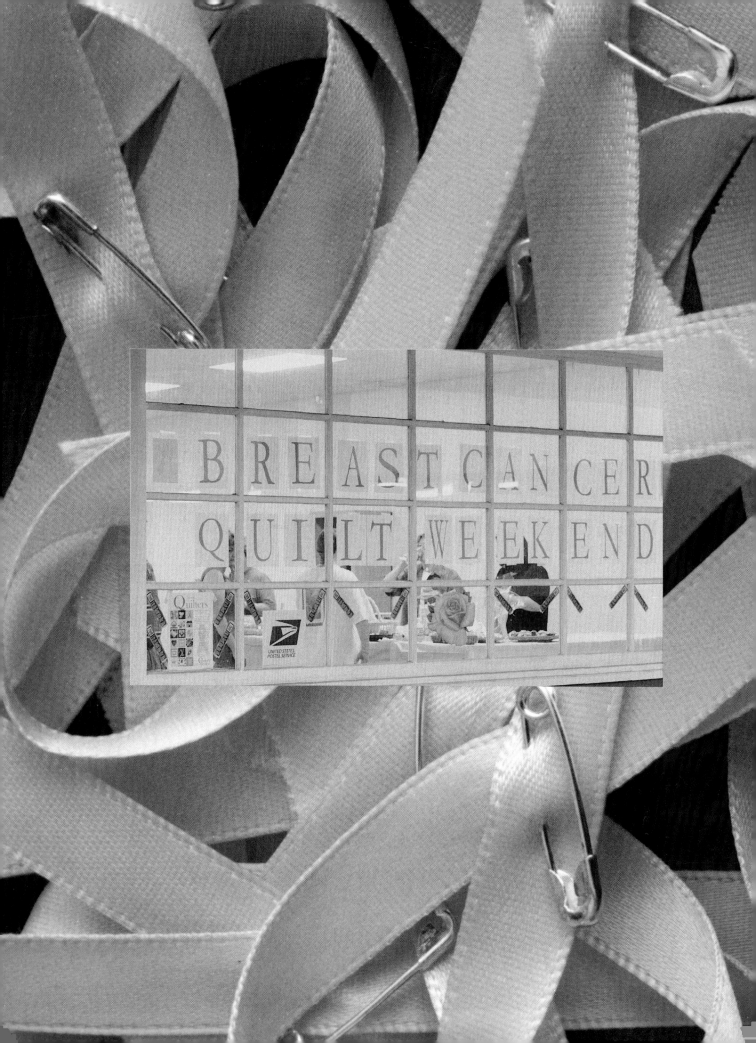

machines going. We always had someone here working."

Many of the volunteers were breast cancer survivors. Sally and Lois put the word out to their customers in general, and to the local chapter of the Susan B. Komen Foundation for Breast Cancer Research. People signed up for four-hour shifts, including an overnight shift on Friday. Work started at six that evening, and continued nonstop until 11 P.M. on Saturday. After an eight-hour break, teams of sewers and pressers reconvened at 7 A.M. Sunday, and continued until ten quilt tops had been assembled at about 5:30 P.M.

One volunteer was Linda Basilio of Watchung, New Jersey. Basilio had a lumpectomy, chemotherapy, and radiation in 1993. "I've been great ever since," says Basilio, an active volunteer for breast cancer research and education, who worked on the quilt assembly on each of the three days. "I have two daughters. They were in middle school when I was diagnosed. You do it for them. I can take anything as long as it doesn't happen to them."

Throughout the weekend, when Basilio wasn't sewing, she distributed breast health information to everyone who came through the door.

"I was very excited," recalls Basilio. "I even hung pink ribbons outside. It was inspiring to see so many people I casually knew, being so personally committed. I always give a huge amount of credit to those who have no immediate connection to breast cancer, but give their time and energy. But when you're a survivor, you take your participation in something like this differently. It was a special camaraderie to meet other survivors. We were hugging each other and crying. We were so grateful to be alive, and very glad to be able to give something back."

i have just learned to sew not quite a year ago ☺ i have learned from my mother, Mary. she _is_ a breast cancer survivor. i absolutely am hooked on quilts. mom smiles with a tear of joy in her eyes everytime she comes down to see me and goes into my craft room. i am making up for lost time with my mother. i thank the Lord every day, for giving my mom the fight & courage to win over Breast Cancer.

—C.J. Pritchard

My first grandchild is now 6 weeks old - may breast cancer - be a thing of the past - When she is a grandmother.

—Beverly Peitz

My Family helped stitch together my shattered Heart After my diagnosis of Breast Cancer in 1997. Early detection saved my Life. My mother was diagnosed with Breast Cancer earlier in the year 1997, causing me to get a mamogram. I was 34 years old, married 16 years to a wonderful man, with our 2 year old son as our joy. mother tearfully told me, "Now I can live with having had Breast Cancer because it saved my child". I am honored to have been given the Gift of Life twice.

—Karen Carver Castleberry

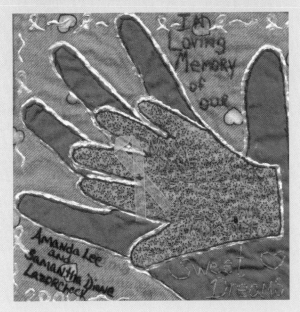

In 1986 my mother was diagnosed with breast cancer. Luckily, it was caught early and she made a complete recovery. In 1996 she was diagnosed with Alzheimer's. This lady has endured two of the most dreaded illnesses.
—Gail Shaffner Kuntz

Unlike Basilio, an experienced quilter, some of the volunteers couldn't sew. They were put to work pressing, and squaring off blocks that weren't quite the right size.

Weeks earlier, B. J. Berti had turned her thoughts to the basic design of the quilts, and after discussions with many people, decided that the blocks should be separated by narrow strips of pink sashing, in a fabric that would also be used for the binding. Berti, Davis, and Griffin selected both a solid fabric and a tiny print and ordered it in three shades of pink—pale, medium, and bright.

Berti had approached the assembly with some trepidation. "I was very concerned about how the quilts were going to look," she reflects. "The response from the club members was so overwhelming, there was no time to take all 3,500 blocks and arrange and place each one. We were still opening envelopes the week before we were scheduled to do the sewing. Now there were all these blocks—how were we going to make sure they looked good together?"

Amazingly, the quilts were laid out, as Berti describes it, "on the fly."

The Quilt Connection staff had lined the entire room with design walls. "It's a felted polyester that allows you to put things up and look at them from a distance, without pinning," explains Davis. "So we could swap things around and shift them to different locales. We started with one quilt, but after a while we were designing two or three at once." Each design began with the selec-

tion of one of the three sashing colors. Rather than going for contrast, Berti and Davis decided to put like with like—the most colorful blocks with the bright pink sashing, the lighter blocks with the soft pastel strips.

"Once we made that decision, the blocks could be grouped into lighter and darker colors, and we just started putting up squares in rows," explains Berti. "We'd grab a handful from the pile, and arrange them on the wall. At the same time, we were making decisions. There were lots of hearts and ribbons and stars, and we made sure those weren't all bunched together. And once you had a number of blocks up, you could move them around for balance and harmony. As we went through the blocks, there was a lot of thought about which ones would complement each other, but there was a lot of randomness, too."

The decisions were made very quickly, often in seconds. But the effect was magic.

"The pink unified everything," says Berti. "And the consideration that we gave as we laid them out—it worked amazingly well."

The walls were not large enough to hold an entire 101" x 105" quilt, so Berti, Davis, and Griffin laid out eight or ten rows at a time.

"Then," Basilio recalls, "I sat down with B. J., whom I'd never met before, and we developed a plan for working on several quilts at once without losing track of which row belonged where. We cut up paper in two-inch squares and made labels." They stacked the blocks one row at a time, pinned a label to the stack—3/5, for example, meant quilt 3, row 5—and handed the stack to a volunteer at a sewing machine. The stack was stitched into a strip with a short piece of

This block is in remembrance of my sister-in-law, Alice Martha Gonzalez. She lost her fight with breast cancer four years ago. She was a daughter, sister, mother, aunt, grandmother, and great-grandmother. We miss her.

—Marie Montoya

sashing sewn between each block. Each completed strip was pressed, then a long strip of sashing was sewn to the bottom edge. Finally, the fifteen rows of twelve blocks each were sewn together, and a quilt top was done.

"I was absolutely amazed when I saw the first one," recalls Berti. "Thrilled. Overwhelmed. We'd chosen the brightest pink sashing for this quilt, and the effect was exciting and dramatic. After looking at all those blocks for so many months as individual things, suddenly it was a quilt! And it looked great. I don't think it was until that moment that I realized the scope of what we were doing."

As each quilt top was completed, it was hung in a vacant storefront next door to the Quilt Connection that Davis's landlord had generously loaned the group. And, for that weekend, the storefront became a focus of the community.

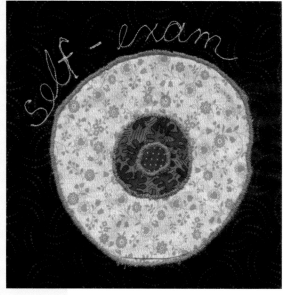

"A postal employee stopped in on Saturday, saw the quilts hanging there, and came back and stood there for the rest of her shift selling the postage stamps that benefit breast cancer research. People were coming in and looking at the quilt tops all day," recalls Davis. "They were fascinated. They touched them. They got chills reading some of the inscriptions. And it really was incredible—the tributes paid by women to other women in the blocks they made."

The biggest surprise to Davis was the unflagging enthusiasm of the volunteers throughout Friday night into Saturday morning. "It was a wonderful experience. As a former nurse married to a

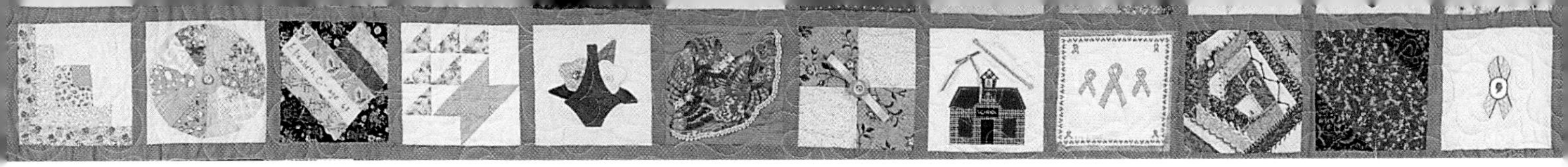

The design of this block incorporates a hug and a kiss from me to all my sisters past, present and future. The yellow square represents the hope we have that there will be a cure.
Love —
Bonnie
3-30-2000

—Bonnie Monsanto

CLAIRE NEAL — Kaiserslautern, Germany

The block is called Joy Bells, and it was chosen because my second cousin, Joy, is a breast cancer sufferer. The watery effects of the fabric were picked to reflect the uncertainty and intangibility of life. Pale pink to depict vulerability and a deep, rich blue to show what strength these women have within.

—Claire Neal

This block was made to remember Aunt Ellen. She was the most wonderful Person. We loved her and miss her, and will never forget her.

—Joy Bailey

doctor, I know what breast cancer is and how devastating it can be," Davis said. "I felt it was the least we could do. Even though B. J. approached us with the concept of 700 blocks, and we ended up with 3,500, I'd do it again."

For Linda Basilio the high point of the weekend came when the ten quilts were done. (The remaining four were later assembled by individual volunteers, including Basilio.) "It was a monumental moment, all of our hands on the quilt as we carried the last one over to the space next door. And when you saw the entire room, all the walls, floor to ceiling, papered with these quilts right next to each other—it was overwhelming—all these women who'd donated their materials, their time, their thoughts.

"When you're first diagnosed with breast cancer, you feel so isolated and alone. I'd made many connections since that time, but this made me feel part of a bigger picture in a different way. It was a complex mix of emotions. You're lucky to be the survivor, but you feel very strange. There are too many people, too many squares on these quilts. You don't want anyone else to have to be a member of this club."

THE QUILTING

Berti found fourteen machine quilters who volunteered to sandwich batting between the quilt tops and the backing (a beautiful fabric with a white-on-white pattern of roses) and complete each quilt in a style that was each quilter's personal choice. Berti sewed the binding on the last quilt herself.

"Each of the quilters chose to do something different," comments Berti. "Some quilted each block individually. Others did an all-over pattern. Sue Ewing of Eulea Quilting in Seaton, Illinois, created a pattern and named her quilt 'Hearts Bound by a Pink Ribbon.' Using pink thread, she started quilting the ribbons in the lower right corner, fanning up and diagonally across the quilt to the

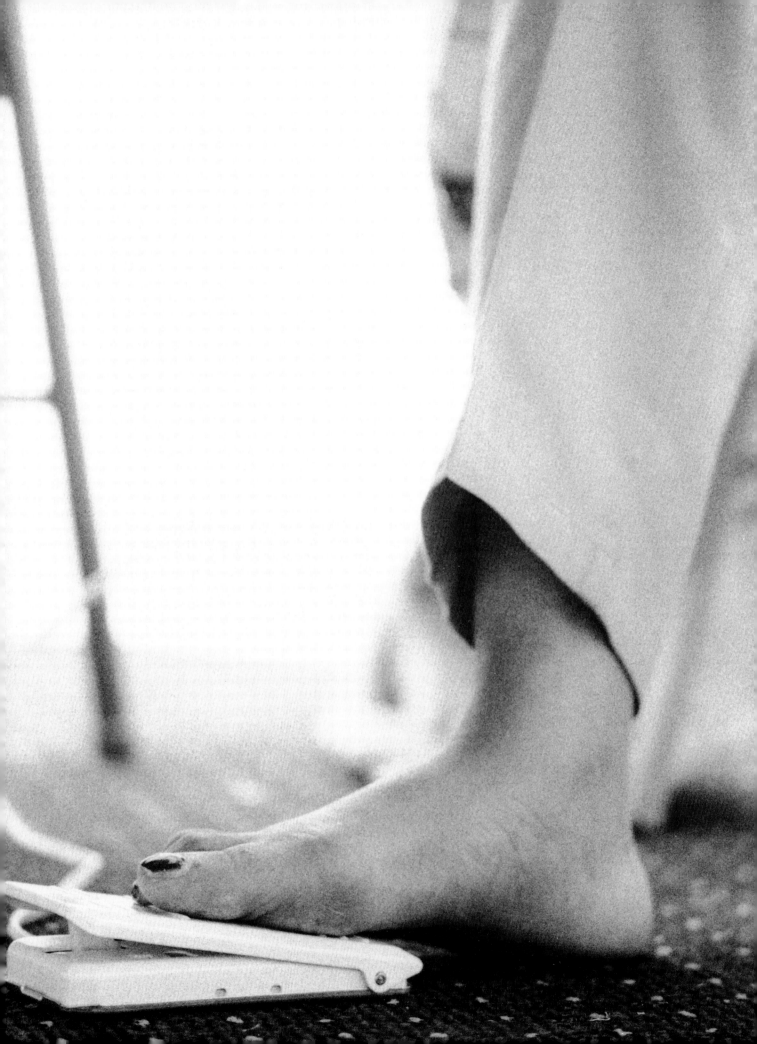

upper left. She entwined roses and hearts around the ribbons. Vines of hearts fill in the rest of quilt."

Cindy Kurpiewski of Lake Hopatcong, New Jersey, heard about the Pink Ribbon project from one of her customers, a breast cancer survivor who's also a Quilt Connection customer, and agreed to submit her name.

"The quilt just came to my house in a box, with no instructions—and I was absolutely in awe of it. First, the size itself"—the Pink Ribbon quilt is the largest Kurpiewski has ever quilted—"it was immense. And there were so many little squares, it took me a while to figure out what I was going to do. Often, I don't know what I'm going to do until the quilt is on the machine."

Kurpiewski used a Gammill Classic twelve-foot long-arm machine for the project, and made herself a couple of rules: "Out of respect," she says, "I decided I wouldn't cross over anyone's name or a pink ribbon with stitching. That gave me some parameters. I chose a deep pink thread that matched the sashing and just did random loops, and once it got going, it just seemed to flow. It took me several days. Then I did the binding as well. So it was in my lap for a long time. Sometimes it was very sad. But I'd gladly do it again. It really brought home how breast cancer touches everyone. It is everywhere."

The Pink Ribbon quilt wasn't the first community quilt Kurpiewski had finished, but she found it very special. "Even though I'd done a quilt for a school, where everyone made a block, this was different because of all the hands that had touched it. Each one of those blocks represented someone's life. There was one with a person's name and age—27. Every time I was near that one, I said, 'Oh my gosh, that's way too young!'

"As I moved through the quilt, it changed constantly. Each block was different. I started at the top, working from left to right, and it was like reading. When you roll it, about every eighteen inches, and the next part is exposed, it was like turning a page. Each time I'd turn it, I'd look at all the blocks as I went along and read them. Which is not something I often do with a quilt. They don't usually have names and ages. But there was always a feeling. There was something to read even in all the blocks that had no words."

THE QUILT BLOCKS

"...Each stitch I did by hand with love"
—Anne Tucker Blake

When B. J. Berti invited Crafter's Choice members to contribute blocks for breast cancer awareness, she gave few limitations, asking only for 6½" squares made of 100% cotton, prewashed and pressed, that "incorporate the color pink somewhere to reflect our theme." These simple parameters gave women of all backgrounds and skill levels the opportunity to create something unique and beautiful.

To the surprise of Crafter's Choice staff, most of the women who contributed blocks sent notes along with them. These brief messages, as much as the blocks themselves, bear witness to love, loss, courage, joy, and hope. The notes honor daughters, mothers, grandmothers, sisters, cousins, aunts, in-laws, stepmothers, childhood friends, and best friends who succumbed to breast cancer or courageously survived it. Many contributors tell the story of their

In memory of my mother Jean Jellema
who taught me how to sew.

—Joy Bailey

To honor my mother Ernestine, a breast Cancer survivor + my aunt Eunice who is still fighting the disease.

—Janet S. Bissell

April 11, 2000

This is my way of showing my thanks to all of The people who have given me loving support AND helped me to Recover from Breast Cancer: My husband and family, my friends, my work colleagues, other cancer fighters, my doctors & nurses.

—Loretta D. Betz

This block is made in honor of the bravest woman I've ever known, my mom, Christine Glynn. The appliqued circle represents the hole in my heart since her battle ended in 1976.

—Diana Glynn Ahrendt

own struggle with the disease. In the blocks themselves, the range of creativity, imagination, and feeling is as broad and varied as the circumstances of the women who made them. "Each person's contribution is unique," says Berti. "Every time I look at the quilts, I see something else."

Who Made Them?

Women who describe themselves as beginning quilters, first-timers, and "non-quilters" made extraordinary contributions. They are stitched side by side with those of professionals, including Mimi Dietrich, who contributed to this volume and whose book, *Pink Ribbon Quilts: A Book Because of Breast Cancer*, was a major inspiration for the Crafter's Choice Pink Ribbon project.

Squares came from all over the U.S. and more than a dozen foreign countries, from people of all ages and ethnic backgrounds. Children made them. An eight-year old, Sarah Philamalee from Mohawk, Michigan, may have been the youngest contributor. Blocks from Girl Scouts troops and troubled teens from a group home appear in the quilts, along with the stitchery of women in their eighties who've been quilting for half a century or more—some of whom have survived breast cancer for decades.

Carol Wahl, past president of Oak Run Quilters in Ocala, Florida, was one of many quilt club leaders who organized group contributions. "Many of our members have had breast cancer or have known people who had it," says Wahl. "The response from the group was very, very strong." Wahl herself lost her mother to breast cancer, and has

My block is in honor of my mother, Barbara Dougherty, who had a mastectomy on February 15, 2000. Thankfully, she is cancer free and doing well. I am a beginning hand quilter. When I realized the top sides of my heart were not perfect, I thought that my mom's not even and matched anymore either, but who cares, she's here and that's just perfect in my eyes.

—Robin Bean

Save The Date

The Fifth Annual
Pink Tie Ball

October 27, 2001
6:00pm

West Orange Armory
Pleasant Valley Way • West Orange, NJ

Proceeds to benefit the North Jersey Affiliate of
The Susan G. Komen Breast Cancer Foundation

several friends who were diagnosed with the disease. "It was kind of a pull-and-tug at the heart as I was assembling the blocks to go out," she recalls. "And I was so touched by the sentiment that came out in people's stories. You work with a bunch of women for a long period of time and you think you know everything about them and then this comes along . . ." The Oak Run Quilters' squares have been incorporated into several different quilts.

The largest entry from an individual came from Ruth A. Price, whose block appears below. Price contributed eighty-seven blocks dedicated to the women she's cared for in twenty years as a cancer nurse. "Each one was made with a piece of my heart," said Price, who inscribed the patient's first name and her age at diagnosis on each square. The letter she sent appears on the following page.

Feb 28, 2000

Dear Crafter's Choice:

Enclosed you will find many quilt squares with first names and
the age at diagnosis. These are women I've taken care of in my
20 years of cancer nursing. Unfortunately, they are only a
fraction of the breast cancer patients I have cared for.

When I first started in nursing in the 1970's, I rarely saw a
breast cancer patient under the age of 60. By the time I went
into cancer nursing, in 1980, I was finding more women being
diagnosed in their 40's and 50's. We always wondered if if was
just better and earlier diagnostics, or a trend.

Into the 1990's, I seem to be seeing more women in their 30's,
and down into their 20's. Now, we're all wondering; "is this a
trend or an environmental disaster?"

I decided to make the squares in heart shapes, because of the
heart all these women have. I could just have easily made
weapon-shaped squares, because of the growing intensity these
women are showing in the fight against breast cancer. As one of
my patients so aptly put it; "I don't want to wear a pink ribbon
like some girl, I want to wear one of those old battle-axes that
the knights used to slay dragons with."

I wish I could honor every single patient I've ever taken care of
with breast cancer, but I think if my memory were that good, I
would have had to make 1000 squares; I think that would have
broken my spirit as well as my heart.

I won't retire for another 15 years. I would really love it if I
became a non-necessity before then. My prayer for the new
century is that cancer nurses and cancer doctors all go the way
of the dinosaurs.

I hope that with the ages on these quilt squares, every woman or
girl child who see's it will realize that no age is exempt; I hope
you're never too young to get it, or too old to get it. I hope
every man who see's this quilt will realize that if he finds a
lump on the breast of the woman he loves, he can show that love
by dragging her to the nearest mammography center as fast as he
can. I hope every mother will teach her daughters to do breast
self exam, and I hope men learn to become more aware of their
potential role in detecting lumps, and supporting their women
through all aspects of care, including attending support groups
with them.

I hope you can use all the squares. Each one was made with a
piece of my heart.

Ruth A. Price

This exceptionally lovely three-dimensional block has a different name embroidered on each ribbon. The ribbons, in three shades of pink, stand for different experiences relating to breast cancer.

A few contributors honored fathers with breast cancer. Mary J. Cannon dedicated her block to her parents, who *both* had breast cancer. Cinda Kahl (top right) dedicated a block each to surgeon Jane Kurtz and oncologist Vera Rose who, Kahl wrote, "fight the battle every day."

Some blocks were made by second wives of breast cancer widowers, like the block (bottom left) made by Pat VanBrandenburg, and the one below right from Diane Miller Divine.

Cinda Kahl's block honors health-care professionals who "fight the battle every day."

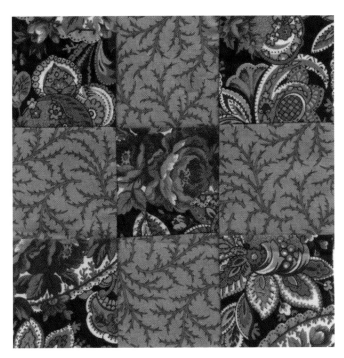

This block is in memory of Barbara VanBrandenburg, who lost her life to breast cancer in May of 1998, after an eleven-year struggle. She left behind her husband, Greg, and two children. Greg and I were married last year, and we thought it fitting to send in [this and other] blocks as a tribute representing each of her family members. We selected the fabrics and designs together.

—Pat VanBrandenburg

A tree for my forester husband who lost his first wife to breast cancer. The background is made of some fabric I think was hers.

—Diane Miller Divine

In a very few words, some messages evoke a vivid picture of a life, such as this note from Barbara Acchino, of Red & White Quilters (right): "Made to honor breast cancer survivor Doris Alice Hadler, my mom. Churn Dash symbolizes Mom's emotions soothed by her many flowers that she had to 'dash' back to tend. She had two cancer surgeries at ages eighty-three and eighty-four followed by radiation. She will be ninety-two in May and is still making quilts."

So, too, does the message from Mary Anttila about her sister; Anttila's block appears below: "Made for my sister Karen who has breast cancer. She loves to collect angels, so I made this angel for her. She also loves her flower gardens and is the single mother of two adopted children from India."

I designed this first block entry in the fall of 1999 when it looked like I would have my first clean year. Today, I'm recovering from mastectomy, but still hopeful of victory.
—Sherry Carlton

Holding Me Together. In February 2000, I designed this second block entry while waiting in my doctor's office for confirmation of a recurrence in my battle against breast cancer that began in December 1996 and would claim my left breast on April 3, 2000. Every "warrior princess" fights her own battle no matter how it compares to the battles of others. We all share the scars and the pain of lives forever changed and lost. To Victory.
—Sherry Carlton

Feistiness, determination, and celebration characterize the statements made by survivors who contributed blocks to honor themselves. "This square carries the fabric I used for my 'chemo quilt,'" wrote Louise Daenick. "During my chemo, I quilted my quilt from June to November 1991. Fully recovered now and in remission!"

And Irene Jones writes, "This block celebrates five years since my surgery for breast cancer. It represents the various colors as you travel the road from the day you find out you have cancer, through the many fears, treatments, and finally the realization you will survive and life is good!"

Sherry Carlton charted the course of her illness in real time as she created two blocks, seen at top left and below.

Helen was my mother. She died when I was nineteen. I have been holding back the tears for twenty-three years not willing to face the pain of her being gone. Thanks for letting me say goodbye.
—Bonnie Rhoby

There are a number of enemies in the breast cancer battle apart from the disease itself. One is the chill of isolation newly diagnosed women describe—and some never overcome. Another is silence, which we fight every time a pink ribbon quilt is displayed, and against which each woman who stitched a block contributed ammunition. Perhaps most devastating: feelings of helplessness in the face of our own illness or the suffering of someone we love. To do *something*—even stitching our feelings into a quilt block—when we're overwhelmed by the sense there's *nothing* we can do helps heal the spirit. Perhaps this is why so many women spoke of gratitude to Crafter's Choice for the "opportunity" to contribute a square—whether this meant to express emotions, share pride, or simply to do one more thing for a beloved mother, sister, or friend long gone.

Susan Radke embodies this with the words she contributed: "In memory of my mother, Joan Robinson, who died in 1997 from breast cancer. I miss her so much. This block gave me so much pleasure to make for her." So, too, does Bonnie Rhoby, whose quilt block appears at left.

Each quilt, with all its pieces, speaks volumes about women's relationships and the importance of our emotional bonds—severed by death, strengthened by adversity, mourned deeply and daily, treasured forever. The power of mother/daughter bonds speaks for itself, a sentiment best expressed by Karen Carver Castleberry, who wrote: "Early detection saved my life. My mother had been diagnosed with breast cancer the same year, causing me to get a mammogram. I was thirty-four. Mother told me, 'Now I can live with having breast cancer because it saved my child.' I am honored to have been given the gift of life twice."

Life is not always perfect,
Nor is my quilt square;
But if the heart is at
    the center of life,
As it is in the center of
    my quilt square,
Each day's great and important.

—Julie Davidson

Susan Steppler, Winnipeg, Manitoba, Canada

Thank you for the opportunity to do something
to help towards honouring the people who have
been touched by breast cancer.

My family has also experienced the fear of
discovering how it feels to have someone you
love find a lump in their breast. My quilt
block represents the luck we had when we
found it was benign.

This is for those who were not as lucky as we
were.

—Susan
Steppler

I have made my quilt block to honor
my niece, Melinda Massa-Fuller, of
Bronx, NY. She had a lumpectomy
in Jan. 1999, went through 6 months
of chemotherapy and 7 weeks of radiation. She kept a positive attitude
through all and has become a strong
survivor. She is 40 years old.
We both thank Crafter's Choice for the
opportunity to be a part of this
wonderful project.

—Katherine M. Doan

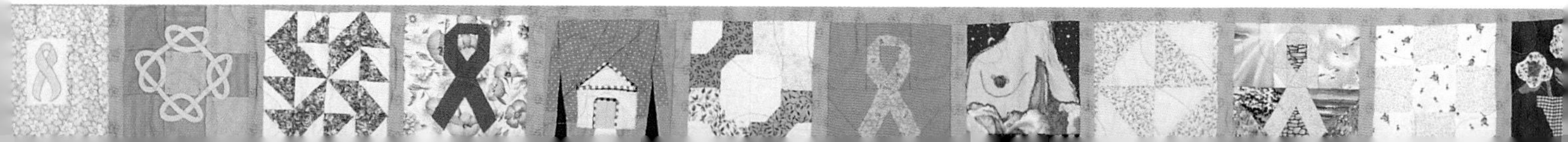

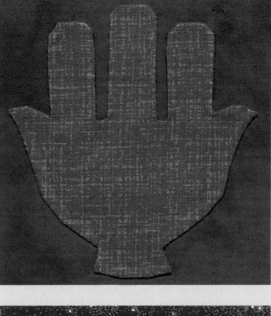

Barbara Longsworth

Kuwait

This block is made
in honor of the
bravest woman I've
ever known, my
mom, Christine
Glynn. The
appliquéd circle rep-
resents the hole in
my heart since her
battle ended in 1976.
—Diana Glynn
Ahrendt

In loving memory of my
beautiful mother, Helen Tucker.
She died of breast cancer in
March 1984. I chose the fabrics
and colors because not only were
they her favorite colors but the
blue is like her sparkling eyes
and the rose like her cheeks. We
used to tease her and say she
could be a model for Mrs. Santa
Claus. Each stitch I did by hand
with love.
—Anne Tucker Blake

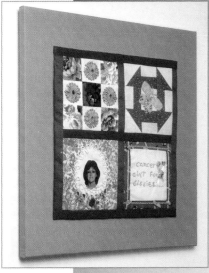

My block is called "Broken Pieces." I have had cancer beginning when I was nineteen. I am now fifty. I have had cancer in many places and have gone through radiation treatments. By the grace of God, I am still alive and have all my hair and most of my body parts. I pray for all who send in blocks for this quilt. I pray for this quilt and for what it stands for. I hope I get to see this quilt one day.

—Belinda Davis

This block was created in memory of Mabel Chan who died after a twelve-year battle with breast cancer. She walks in the forest that the creek flows through. The Rocky Mountains covered in snow are painted pink as the sun sets. These walks provided Mabel with calm that helped her survive long enough to see her sons into adulthood.

—Maxine Adshead

This block is for my mom, who died from breast cancer in 1992. With the exception of the muslin backing, the fabrics I used are all cut from my mom's blouses.

—Sherry Rich

Fabrics marketed to help support breast cancer research were used by a number of contributors. Other choices reflect lives lived and loved ones lost, as Cindy Bajis writes: "In memory of my sister, Rebekoh Lynn Davis, who lost her life to breast cancer in 1992. The ladybug print is from the dress of her first grandchild, whom she never met."

Doris Jenkins also told us about the fabric she used: "This material is from a quilt I made for my granddaughter who is four now. She had just turned three when I had a lumpectomy. Hopefully with research my little one will never need to go through breast cancer." And Joan Gallagher-Badami described her material

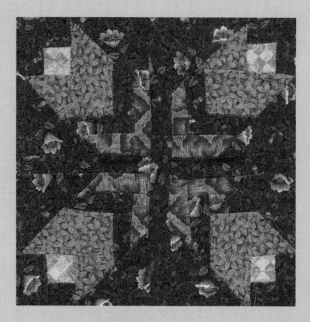

What is real...
What is Lasting
is created
by Hand...
given with
Heart

as well: "My block honors the memory of my great aunt, Lillian Germeyer, who died of breast cancer in 1939. She was thirty-four years old. The pink ribbon is partially hidden to signify the taboo of even discussing the subject at that time. I have used vintage fabric of that era from my collection."

HOPE ABOUNDS

Contributors mentioned the color yellow in their comments at least as frequently as they referred to pink. Most often, yellow is associated with hope. Many women, like Karina Berger (see page 81) and Chrissy Ahrendt Walker (see below) also chose round, golden suns and the color yellow as symbols of hope. Sue Walters embroidered a sun on her pastel crazy-quilt square in memory of her mother, who was diagnosed with breast cancer at age thirty-nine, and died at age fifty-one. "I was diagnosed in 1999. My prognosis is good. The flowers on the block represent my mom, the buttonhole wheel the ups and downs of dealing with this." (See page 113 for Sue Walters's block.)

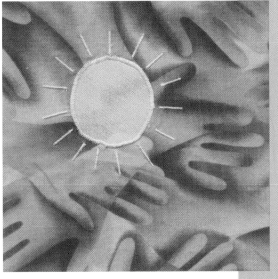

The sun is her strength and the hands represent her reaching out to others. She is a survivor.
—Chrissy Ahrendt Walker

Many women sent powerful statements of hope without ever mentioning the word. This is Karen Barthman's note: "My sister-in-law, Nancy Barthman, is a breast cancer survivor of thirty years and this square is sent in her honor. "

From Elizabeth Christhilf: "I have been a survivor for twelve years. I am now eighty-six and feel fine."

And from Carla Arthur: "This block is in honor of my grandmother, Delphine, a breast cancer survivor. The nine patches represent her three children, my mom's three children and my three children, great health to us all!"

Others expressed hope symbolically in their designs, such as the two blocks that appear on page 71.

The two ribbons, entwined, are for Anne and Margaret Richardson, mother and daughter survivors of breast cancer from 1983 and 1998. The yellow background signifies vibrant life and hope—we are still here!

—Anne Richardson

I am a beginner quilter but wanted to do this for my son-in-law. This block is in memory of his mother, Barbara, who died from breast cancer. She loved art and nature. She was an officer in the Fraternal Order of Eagles. The butterfly has become a symbol for breast cancer. It also represents Barbara's flight and relief from pain. The heart tells of our love for her.

—Sharon L. Dougherty

Also representing hope are butterflies, a common theme in the quilts. Some contributors also refer to the butterfly's association with death and the transition to the afterlife. To others they symbolize emerging from the chrysalis of cancer treatment as a survivor—freedom and rebirth in this world.

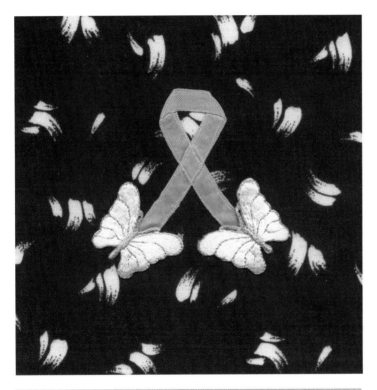

Our quilt block displays butterflies that represent how delicate, unique and beautiful we all are. We are a teen female facility and are excited to be part of this project which has helped us be more aware of this illness and the importance of early detection. Our butterflies symbolize the day all women can spread their wings and be free of this disease.
—Margaret R. Harvey
Harriet Tubman
Residential Center

Yes, to small miracles. Yes, to never giving up. Yes, to facing life each day! My friend Lorna had breast cancer six years ago. She is a miracle; she never gave up and survived. She lives her life to the fullest. I honor her courage and strength.
—Charlotte Witwer

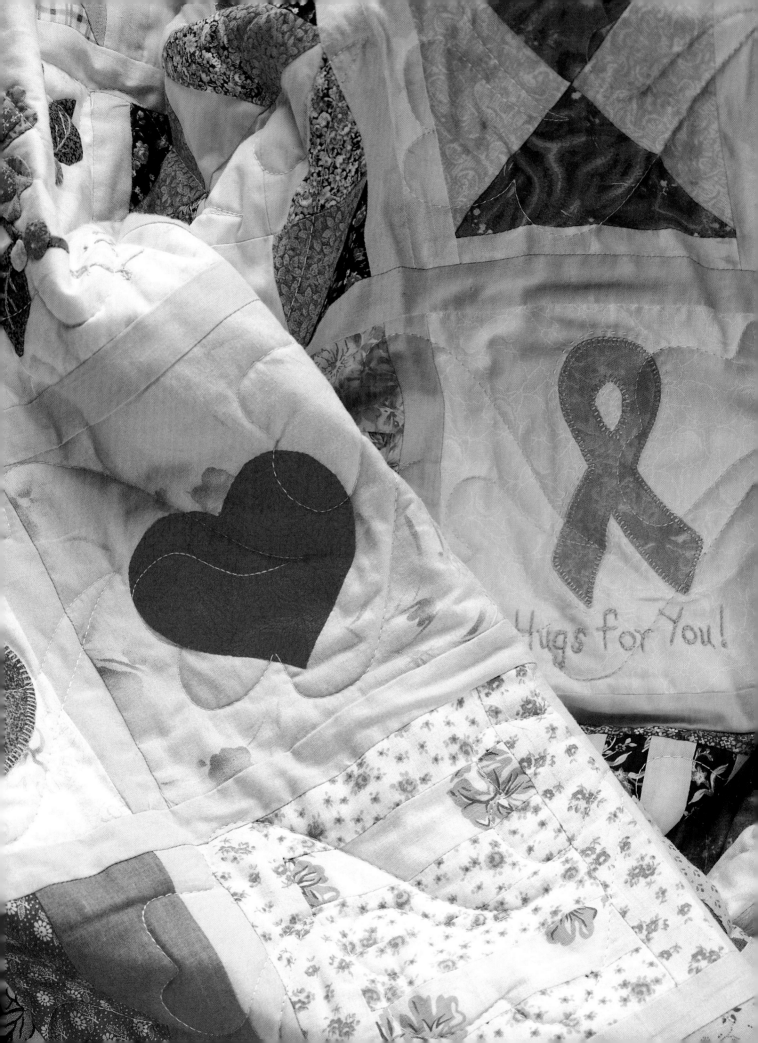

Hugs for You!

I cross-stitch and Mom quilts; we made our first quilt together in 1994. And, each year since we have made another.

Mom is a four year (and counting) breast cancer survivor. Your call for blocks seemed like a perfect project for us.

—Patricia L. Pieti
and
Lisa Pieti Opie

This is in honor of all breast cancer victims & survivors, including my quilter mentor, Ruby.

This is to encourage medical personnel to cure breast cancer & all cancers, keeping HOPE in all our hearts.

Peggy 2000

—Margaret H. Sparks

THIS BLOCK IS TO HONOR MY SISTER FLORA POWERS. ACCEPTING THE FACT SHE IS NO LONGER WITH US HAS REALLY BEEN HARD. NOT ONLY DID SHE LEAVE US SHE LEFT 7 CHILDREN, 5 GIRLS &2 BOYS , I'M SURE KNOWING THEIR MOTHER WILL BE REMEMBERED IN A BLOCK ON A QUILT WILL MEAN ALOT TO THEM.

—Clara Burney

Star of Hope. Dee Kelley will always remain in our hearts. Thank you for helping to celebrate her life on earth and keep her memory alive.
—Kim Stickney

The star is a powerful symbol of hope in many cultures. *Friendship Star, Star of Hope, North Star, Ohio Star,* and *Christmas Star* are among the traditional star patterns stitched into the quilts.

HEARTS, FLOWERS, AND RIBBONS

It's in hearts, flowers, and ribbons that the color pink is most often expressed. Sometimes all three appear in a single block. The flowers contributors chose, executed in patchwork, embroidery, and appliqué, ranged from traditional roses, violets, and pansies to a complex and beautifully rendered painted trillium.

I made this quilt square in memory of my friend Joan Greenblatt, who died of breast and brain cancer in 1982. I was also diagnosed with breast cancer in 1999. I selected the star and moon background fabric for my square because, early in the morning after I was diagnosed, the sky was full of stars when I went out to get the newspapers. It's very rare to see stars in the Los Angeles sky, so I took this as a good omen for my own prognosis.
—Diana K. Britt

I decided to put most of the pinks in the flower. I drew hearts in hands to represent all of us women who have the potential of getting cancer—a fear I have had all my life. I put the dove with the sprig of a plant to give us HOPE. It reminds me of Noah's Ark and what they overcame. We need to keep the hope and faith and pray to God to get through this.
—Irene Bowie

The heart material is a symbol that no woman is alone in this fight. The flowers are a sign of new beginnings.
—Crystal Hinch

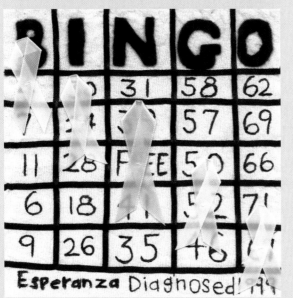

Esperanza Diagnosed! 199

Thinking about breast cancer, my subconscious drew this pattern with no curves or parallels, but with "rays" and a suggestion of a star. I had a mastectomy and chemo seven years ago, and my Mom just died of ovarian cancer. What I have learned is that a cancer patient must change in order to live, and live to change.

—Barbara King

"Treatment days are gray. Remission is pink. Two years and counting," wrote Vicki Brodkin, and Chris Correa submitted her quilt square with this note: "For my friend, Kathy Hutchinson, who is a two-time breast cancer survivor and doing well. The block is a traditional log cabin. I used shades of pink with the lightest at the center, so it looks like a light at the end of a tunnel." The most

The color pink is for breast cancer awareness. I am a survivor. I had a left mastectomy seventeen years ago. The color green is for life, as are the roses. The line through the white is for continuity.
—Karin Burghart

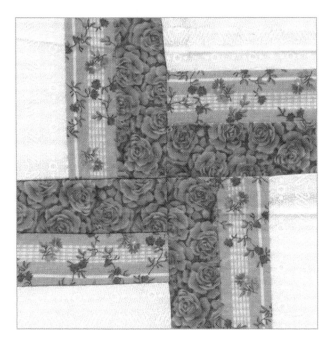

The block is called Joy Bells, and it was chosen because my second cousin Joy is a breast cancer sufferer. The watery effects of the fabric were picked to reflect the uncertainty and intangibility of life. Pale pink to depict vulnerability and a deep, rich blue to show what strength these women have within.
—Claire Neal

The rose, the symbol for breast cancer research. The daffodil, the symbol for cancer research. The sunrise symbolizes a new dawn bringing hope for a cure.

—Karina Berger

Violets represent hope for a cure. Three violets represent my granddaughters, Emily, Krissy, and Shayne. I am a seven-year breast cancer survivor.

—Cecilia Huotari

This block is made in memory of my sister, Charlotte Custer, who died of breast cancer at the age of forty-two. The three hearts represent her three children who were left behind, the oldest being just eight years old. Our father also died of breast cancer at the age of sixty-three.

—Carol Sue Kern

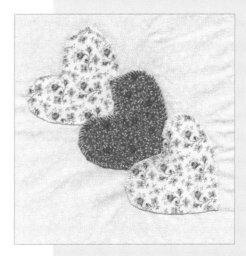

This block is made to honor the many women friends and Medical Mission Sisters who have died with breast cancer and those who still live with it. The pink is to remember their disease, the red to commemorate their great courage. The kite in the sky is to remember their spirits which soared so much higher and further than their disease allowed them.

—Myrtle E. Keller

important element in the quilts is the color pink. While messages of hope express one aspect of the generous, uplifting spirit of the quilts, the unifying pink imbues them with joy. Numerous blocks include some version of pink ribbon that first came to symbolize breast cancer awareness when the Susan G. Komen Foundation gave one to each runner in the 1991 Race for the Cure in New York City. Despite the prevalence of the familiar loop of pink ribbon, however, it's the sashing that really creates the flow of ribbons of pink on each quilt.

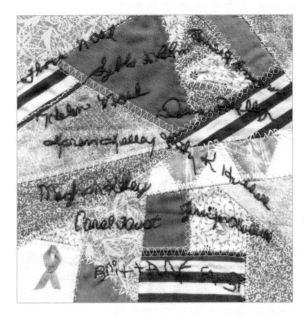

The pink sashing further links the pink elements that occur in every square. "The pink in the blocks is not always that obvious," Crafter's Choice's Berti points out. The central figure in appliquéd embroidered blocks, a rose or a butterfly, might be pink, but that color is dominant in only a few blocks; more have just a hint of pink in one fabric in a complex patchwork, or a tiny pink flower on a contrasting ground. "There's absolutely every shade, from pale to nearly red or purple," remarks Berti. "It's very interesting, the choices people made, and how they interpreted pink. The range is huge."

From a distance, each quilt is like a garden of pink flowers, each block a blossom, with all the nuances of floral variety—from the variegation of dianthus and Sweet William to the brilliance of coral bell, geranium, peony, and rose.

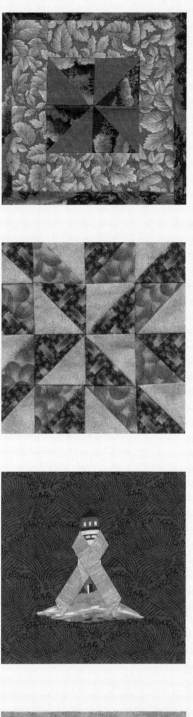

The Pink Ribbon Quilts gain much of their power from the dynamic juxtaposition of finely wrought traditional squares like the two squares at top right with unique, surprising work including a range of unusual images from the kite (see page 82) to the lighthouse at right. Whimsy and humor brighten the picture. Sylvia Almack of Forgotten Corner Quilters stitched a dashing patchwork hat into her block (pictured at bottom right), and wrote: "Chemotherapy treatment is an opportunity to wear all those funky hats you never thought you could." In a more primitive but equally artful and expressive style, the block created by Marcia Reed at bottom center features an appliqué of a jolly Raggedy Ann-style figure whose outstretched hands extend beyond the edges of the block—a woman she describes as "reaching out to help others."

Many of the individual blocks are complete works of art in themselves. Mabel Chan, who survived breast cancer for twelve years, "long enough to see her sons into adulthood" is honored in the extraordinary, painterly mountain scene stitched by Maxine Adshead (see page 66). The block contributed by Barbara Coppack actually *is* a painting (bottom left)—an evocative portrait of a pensive woman wearing a pink bonnet and holding a bouquet of flowers. "The woman has just been told she has breast cancer," wrote Coppack. "She wants to be alone and to decide what to do. The outside world is gray, but the yellow room represents hope of surviving—the fight to live."

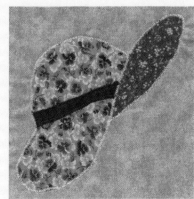

In the tradition of all the quilters who, over the last hundred years or so, have stitched for a cause, Crafter's Choice has donated two quilts to the Susan G. Komen Foundation, where they raised more than $5,000 for breast cancer research at auction. Another quilt, donated to the American Craft Exposition Benefit in Chicago, was purchased by Evanston Northwestern Hospital for $5,000, which was donated to the Evanston Northwestern Breast Cancer Research Institute. The quilt will be displayed in rotation at the hospital's three facilities.

Five quilts have been displayed at the Houston International Quilt Festival. One was shown at the Rockome Gardens Quilt Celebration in Arcola, Illinois, and three were exhibited at the Horry County Museum in Conway, South Carolina, in 2001. Two more were featured at the Machine Quilters Showcase in Springfield, Illinois. Three of the quilts were displayed from May to October 2001 in the Time-Life Building in Manhattan's Rockefeller Center. In addition to the three imposing quilts, the exhibit included eighty individual blocks mounted in panels of four, and accompanied by the powerful written statements from some of the women who created them.

The Pink Ribbon Quilts have a long road ahead of them. No one can predict how much research money they will eventually raise, or in what museums, corporate headquarters, or private residences they will ultimately find homes. But wherever they come to rest for the near future, the Pink Ribbon Quilts are destined to find a place in textile history as distinguished works of American folk art from the turn of the twenty-first century.

—Bibi Wein
June 2002

For my mother, Claire Wein, who lost her battle with breast cancer on Valentine's Day, 1976.

So a child may always be able to bring her mother flowers.
—Carol Steinhauer

Star of Hope. Hope for a cure, a star to show the way.
—Emilie Kimpel

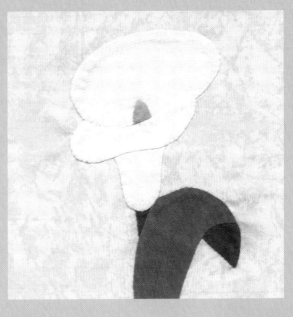

I've had two breast cancers — twelve and eleven years ago. Eight of my close friends and relatives have had breast cancer. Nine close persons! This should not happen. We desperately need to conquer this insidious disease.

My thanks for your help.

My square was made to remember and to honor these nine women — nine women and 286 years of friendship.

2-9-2000

Betty Gow
Log Cabin Quilters' Guild

—Betty Gow

I was inspired to make this quilt block through the memory of a wonderful childhood friend who passed away 10 years ago from breast cancer. She was only 30, and I still can't believe she is gone. I dream about her often, however, so her spirit must be very much alive! Thanks for giving us an opportunity to show our support. Barb

—Barbara Eveleigh

THIS QUILT BLOCK IS FOR MY MOM WHO DIED FROM BREAST CANCER IN 1992.

WITH THE EXCEPTION OF THE MUSLIN BACK, THE FABRICS I USED ARE ALL CUT FROM MY MOM'S BLOUSES, MAKING THIS QUILT BLOCK ESPECIALLY SPECIAL TO ME.

—Sherry Rich

My block is dedicated to Linda, Kristine, and Grace. They are survivors of breast cancer and attend my church. They are beautiful, continue to grow daily, and have kept their roots firmly planted in God's word, just like the flowers depicted in my block.

—Melanie Vaden

DIRECTIONS FOR TWELVE QUILT BLOCKS

BASIC HOW-TO'S 96

PATCHWORK HEART 98

APPLIQUÉ HAT 100

JACOB'S LADDER 102

FOLK ART BOUQUET 105

DOGWOOD IN BLOOM 107

WAVY RIBBON 109

NINE-PATCH HEARTS 111

CRAZY QUILT BLOCKS 113

HUG & KISS 118

DAFFODIL MOSAIC 121

HEART-IN-HAND 125

CHOOSING FABRICS: Use good quality, finely woven, 100% cotton fabric for these blocks. Check your stash for scraps and small amounts; and audition the colors, and patterns and scales of prints by placing them over larger pieces of fabric that will serve as a background. Consider purchasing a fat eighth for this background fabric.

PREPARING YOUR FABRICS: Make sure all your fabrics are washed in warm water and dried to check for colorfastness and to pre-shrink the fabrics. (*Tip*: Place scraps and small pieces of fabric into a mesh bag so they won't clog the drain.) Press the fabrics using spray starch to add extra body, making the fabric pieces easier to cut and handle, and less likely to stretch out of shape when you're working with them. Wait until after the quilt block is assembled and the quilt is completed to wash out this starch, as well as any marks from fabric pencils.

CUTTING: For scissors cutting, use scissors reserved for cutting fabrics. Use craft scissors for cutting out paper patterns or plastic template material.

For rotary cutting, a 6 1/2" square acrylic quilter's ruler can be used for making small cuts, and will be ideal for trimming the completed blocks. Work over a cutting mat, and use a rotary cutter with a sharp blade. For safety's sake, take care to keep fingers away from the rotary blade, and to close the blade when you're not using it.

Keep multiple pieces identified as they are cut, using Post-It notes or placing them on the original pattern.

MACHINE-STITCHING: Be sure your sewing machine is in good working order and equipped with a sharp, new needle—70/10 is a good size for piecing. Use a standard weight (50) sewing thread—cotton, poly, or a cotton-covered polyester. If you are piecing lots of different colors in your project, a neutral beige or gray should blend with all your fabrics. For accuracy in piecing, it is important to make consistent 1/4" seam allowances; use a patchwork foot or a seam guide to help you accomplish this. Pin to secure pieces, but substitute basting stitches or remove the pins as you go; avoid sewing over them.

HAND APPLIQUÉ: A #10 sharps needle is recommended for all but the most experienced stitchers, who may prefer a #11. Work with 18" strands of thread, using a color to match the appliqué. Make a knot at the end, and start by bringing the needle up from the back of the appliqué at the marked line, so that the knot will be hidden under the appliqué piece. Turn the edges of the appliqué to the wrong side, and make tiny blindstitches through the threads of fabric right along the fold and down into the background fabric. Bring the needle up again 1/8" away for the next blindstitch. After the last stitch, bring the thread to the back, make a tiny knot close to the surface, pass the needle under the appliqué piece for ¹/₂", and tug on the thread to bury the knot. Clip the thread end close to the surface of the fabric.

PRESSING: Use a hot, dry iron for most pressing. For work with fusible web, protect your work, the iron, and the ironing board by using a pressing sheet. For most piecing, press the seam first as it was sewn, to set the seam, then unfold one piece and press the seam allowances to one side. To avoid bulk, press seam allowances open. For appliqué, press over a padded surface, and use a press cloth. If a block has become distorted or misshapen, pin it onto the ironing board in the proper shape, steam-press, and let the block dry completely before removing it from the ironing surface.

TRIMMING THE BLOCK: The directions for these 6" finished blocks—6¹/₂" including seam allowances—usually call for working on a background piece 7 or 7¹/₂" square, or adding framing strips that are wider than mathematically necessary. Starting with this extra margin allows for the possibility that the block will shrink a bit from a lot of appliqué stitching, or that seam allowances will be a hair wider than the requisite ¹/₄". Furthermore, as you work on a block, excessive handling may leave it with raveled edges. Trimming the block at the end guarantees a consistent size for combining with blocks of the same or different design as well as a clean cut edge for joining.

Before assembling your blocks into a quilt, trim them to size: 6¹/₂" square, which includes ¹/₄" seam allowance all around. Make sure the design is centered. A clear acrylic quilter's ruler 6¹/₂" square or larger makes the job easy and accurate, because you can see through it to center the design and to ensure that the grain lines run parallel to the edges. Use this tool with a rotary cutter and work over a cutting mat. Alternatively, use a T-square and pencil or fabric-marking pencil to mark the cutting line for the block, and scissors-cut out along the cutting lines of the block, leaving ¹/₄" seam allowances all around.

FINISHING THE QUILT: To make a quilt top, arrange your blocks on a large flat surface so you have a flow or balance of color that you like. Separate the blocks with sashing strips as follows (ours are 1¹/₄" in width, including ¹/₄" seam allowance), always pressing the seam allowances toward the sashing strips. First, cut 6¹/₂"-strips and stitch them between blocks on horizontal rows. Measure and cut strips to span the length of each pieced row, and stitch these between rows.

To assemble your quilt, cut out a backing (piece if necessary) and batting slightly larger all around than your quilt top. Lay the backing out smooth on a large, flat surface, taping the edges. Spread the batting smoothly on top, and center the quilt top over that. Baste generously to keep from shifting. Tie, quilt by hand, or machine quilt, as you prefer. Trim, then bind the edges with the same material used in the sashing. Add a quilt label and perhaps a hanging sleeve to the back.

Springtime floral prints of varying scales and a gingham background combine for this country-fresh image of love and remembrance. Combining piecing and appliqué, this block offers a nice opportunity to try both techniques.

What you'll need:
- Fabrics: 7¹/₂" square for background (here, a gingham print); small amounts of 4 floral prints in coordinating colors
- Clear or translucent template plastic
- Fine-tip permanent marker
- Scissors for paper or plastic, and for fabric
- Fabric-marking pencils
- Sewing needle
- Pins
- Sewing thread to match fabrics, or a neutral to blend
- Sewing machine (optional)
- Iron

What to do:

1. Prepare the templates: Trace the lines and the grain arrows of the actual-size heart pattern (shown on the following page) onto a piece of clear template plastic, using a permanent marker. Cut out the pieces along the lines, using craft scissors.

2. Cut out the fabric pieces: Arrange each of the four pieces on a different fabric as follows. Look through the clear or translucent pattern material to position the fabric motifs in a pleasing way, and also, if possible, to align the grain lines with the arrows; be sure to allow for ¹/₄" seam allowances beyond the pattern edges all around. Lightly trace around each template, using a fabric pencil in a color that will contrast. Cut out each piece ¹/₄" beyond the marked line, for seam allowances.

3. Piece the heart: Arrange the pieces into the heart shape, and join the pieces in alphabetical order, as indicated on the original actual-size pattern. Start by positioning piece A and piece B together along their common side, with right sides facing and edges even. Place a pin at the beginning and end of the seam. Stitch by hand or by machine, ¹/₄" from edges. Press the seam allowances toward the darker fabric piece. Add piece C and then piece D in the same way. For a neat V at the top center of the heart, do not stitch into the seam allowance area.

4. Appliqué the heart in place: To center the pieced appliqué on the background fabric, fold both in half vertically and horizontally, crease the fold-lines, and unfold. Matching up the centers and the creases, pin the heart onto the background fabric square. Refer to the Basic How-To's for Hand Appliqué on page 96, and begin at the middle of one side. Work carefully around the curves of the heart to get a smooth edge, and take care to fold the edges in neatly at the bottom angle of the heart.

5. Finishing: Lightly press the block. Referring to the Basic How-To's on page 97, trim the edges of the background fabric square to measure 6½" square, with the heart appliqué centered.

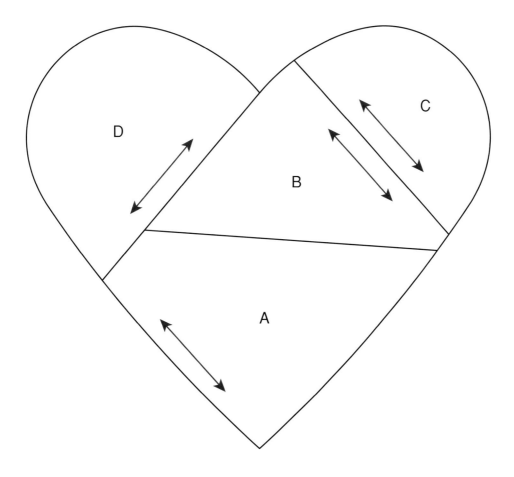

Actual-Size Pattern for Patchwork Heart Appliqué

APPLIQUÉ HAT
by Phyllis L. Jamison-Marcus

This block is to honor Michelle Bogatz Welford. She is the precious sorority sister of my daughter, Heidi. Michelle has breast cancer. We are all praying for her and hoping all her medical treatments go well. We love her.

A hat of some sort is often the accessory of choice for women undergoing medical treatments that lead to hair loss. Making this block is a way to tip your hat in tribute to those who wage their battles with style. If your machine doesn't have a buttonhole stitch, use a zigzag stitch to finish all the appliqué edges.

What you'll need:
- Fabrics: 7¹/₂" square for background (here, a pale monotone); small amounts of floral prints: a monochromatic print (here, rose) for the hat, and a multicolored print for the hatband
- Tracing paper and pencil
- Lightweight fusible web
- Iron and ironing board
- Scissors for paper and fabric
- Fabric-marker
- Sewing machine with zigzag stitch and an open toe foot
- Sewing thread in colors to match and contrast

What to do:
1. Prepare the appliqués: Photocopy the actual-size hat pattern (shown on the following page) or trace it onto a piece of tracing paper. Apply fusible web to the wrong sides of the appliqué fabrics, following the manufacturer's instructions for the web. Pin the hat pattern on the right side of the fusible-backed monochromatic print, and cut along the outside lines.

Next, cut away the single shape of the hat band on the paper pattern. (*Note:* the purple line on the actual-size pattern indicates a line of stitching, not the dividing line of two separate appliqué pieces.) Pin this pattern piece on the right side of the fusible-backed multicolored print fabric, and cut out along the outside lines. To transfer the line of stitching to the hat band, cut the pattern apart along the purple line. Pin one piece on the appliqué piece to correspond, aligning the edges. Using a fabric marker, trace along the cut edge to draw the line shown on the actual-size pattern in purple.

2. Fuse the appliqués in place: Remove the paper backing from each appliqué piece. Measuring carefully, center the hat piece on the background fabric, pinning to secure. Fuse the pieces to the background, removing the pins before you lower the iron onto those areas. Position the hat band on top, and fuse in place.

3. Machine-appliqué the edges: Using thread to match the hat fabric and a buttonhole stitch (narrow blanket stitch), go over the outside edges of the hat, except where it is overlapped by the hat band.

(*Note:* Substitute hand embroidery or machine zigzag stitches if necessary or desired.)

Using a high contrast-color thread, work fine, medium-width zigzag stitches (satin stitch) over the edges and the marked line of the hat band.

4. Finishing: Lightly press the block. Referring to the Basic How-To's on page 97, trim the edges of the background fabric to 6¹/₂" square, taking care to keep the hat centered.

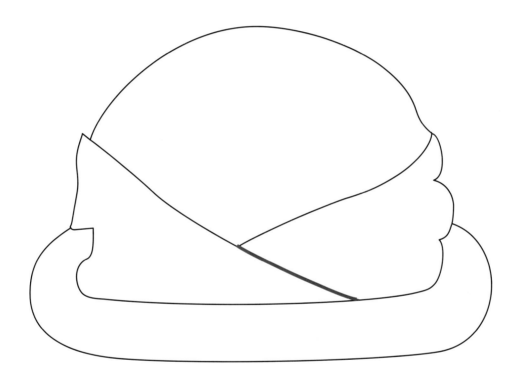

Actual-Size Pattern for the Hat Appliqué

JACOB'S LADDER
by Susan Nycum

This block is to honor a coworker who has recently finished treatment. . . . The Jacob's Ladder is for the hard climb she's had to overcome and the yellow at the top represents the fact that her future will be much brighter!

This classic pattern, called Underground Railroad as well as Jacob's Ladder, combines four-patch mini blocks with triangle squares in a Nine-Patch, or tic-tac-toe setting. Rotary cutting and speed piecing let you ascend this Ladder in a flash, while oversize-cutting and then trimming to fit guarantee perfect results.

What you'll need:
- Fabrics: small amounts of 7 prints; shown here: fuchsia (1), green (2), purple (3), mauve (4), peach (5); scrap of a second mauve print (6) and yellow (7)
- Rotary cutter and cutting mat
- Clear quilter's rulers, 3" x 8" or larger, and 6½" square
- Sewing needle
- Pins
- Sewing thread in a neutral color, to blend
- Sewing machine
- Iron and ironing board

What to do:
1. Oversize-Cutting the Four-Patch Units: Using a quilter's ruler and rotary cutter, cut a 2" x 8" strip along the grain from each of fabrics 1, 2, 3, and 4. In addition, cut two 2" squares from fabric 3, and one each from fabrics 6 and 7.

2. Strip-Piecing: Thread the machine with neutral-colored thread, and set it for a smaller than usual stitch—about 14 stitches per inch. Place a strip of fabric 1 and 2 together with right sides facing, and stitch them together along one long side. Press the seam allowances toward the darker fabric. Lay the joined strips on the cutting mat and use the ruler and rotary cutter to subdivide the strip into 2" segments, cutting perpendicular to the seam and long edges. Repeat this strip-piecing process with fabrics 3 and 4. Also join the squares of fabrics 3 and 6, and fabrics 3 and 7, stitching and pressing in a similar way.

3. Combining the Four-Patch Units: To create a Four-Patch unit, place the segments together in pairs, with the same fabric pieces diagonally opposite each other. Arrange two Four-Patch units with fabrics 1 and 2, one with fabrics 3 and 4, one with fabrics 3, 4, and 6, and one with fabrics 3, 4, and 7. Refer to the photo and the units on the actual-size diagram on page 104 made up of A units.

Position the pairs of segments together with right sides facing and edges even. The pressed seam allowances of each pair should face in opposite directions. To ensure a perfect intersection at the center of each Four Patch, make a tacking stitch that goes through both seams at the center, $1/4$" from the raw edges. Also pin the pieces together at the ends. Stitch, $1/4$" from the raw edges. Press the seam allowances open to avoid bulk.

4. Trim the Four-Patch Units: Using a square quilter's ruler and rotary cutter, trim the unit as follows: Align horizontal and vertical lines on the ruler $1^1/4$" from the edge over the center seams. Rotary cut along the two edges of the ruler. Rotate the Four-Patch unit 180 degrees and repeat the process to trim the other two sides. Repeat on each Four-Patch unit until each of the 5 units is $2^1/2$" square, or 2" square plus $1/4$" seam allowance all around.

5. Creating Oversize Triangle Squares: Using a quilter's ruler and rotary cutter, cut two 4" squares from fabrics 3 and 5. Carefully position non-matching squares together in pairs with right sides facing and edges even. Rotary cut the layered squares diagonally in half. Leaving the layers of each half intact, stitch along the diagonal, $1/4$" from the cut edge. Press the seam to "set" it. Then, with the darker fabric on top, unfold the top layer and press. The seam allowances will be pressed towards the darker fabric.

6. Trim the Triangle Squares: Use a square quilter's ruler and rotary cutter to trim each unit to $2^1/2$" square, taking care to keep the seam running corner to corner.

7. Assemble the block: Arrange the Four-Patch units and triangle squares to match the photo on page 102 and the actual-size diagram on page 104. Stitch the units together into rows; press the seam allowances toward the triangle squares. Position the top and center rows together. Make a tacking stitch to secure the edges right at the matching seams, and pin at either end of this edge. Stitch, $1/4$" from the raw edges. Press the seam allowances open to avoid bulk. Add the bottom row in the same way.

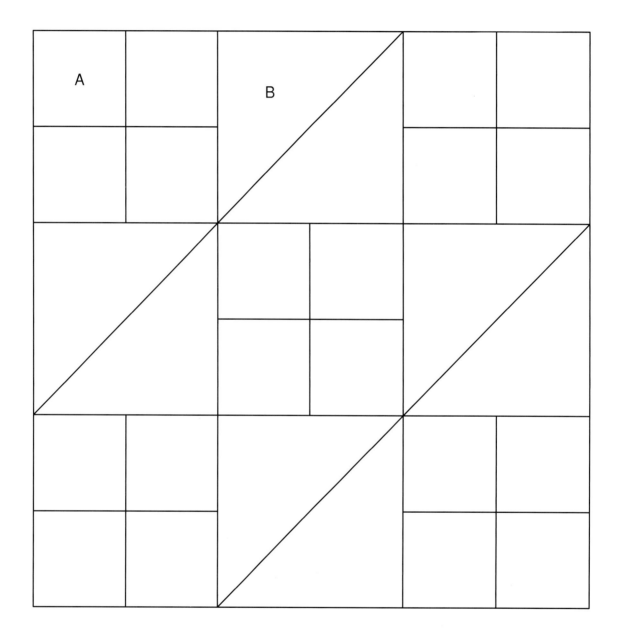

Actual-Size Diagram

FOLK ART BOUQUET
by Leann Herrington

With this handful of pink posies, charm comes by way of simple fused and machine-stitched appliqué. Consider making several blocks, each using the same appliqué shapes in different arrangements.

What you'll need:
- Fabrics: 7½" square for background (here, a hand-dyed red); small amounts of 4 pink prints and 2 green fabrics
- Tracing paper
- Light box or sunny window
- Masking tape
- Fabric-marking pencil in color to contrast with background fabric
- Lightweight fusible web
- Iron and ironing board
- Scissors for paper and fabric
- Sewing machine with zigzag stitch and an open toe foot
- White sewing thread

What to do:
1. Mark the background: Photocopy the actual-size pattern or trace it onto a piece of tracing paper. Tape the paper on top of a light box or onto a sunny window. Center the oversize square of background fabric wrong side down on top, matching the grain lines of the fabric with the short dash lines around the design (which represent the stitching lines for the block when it is assembled). Keep the fabric from shifting with a bit of tape. Using a fabric-marking pencil (white or silver works well on red fabric), lightly mark the entire appliqué design as well as the dash lines on the fabric. Carefully remove the tape and set aside the marked background fabric and the pattern.

2. Prepare the appliqués: Apply fusible web to the wrong sides of the appliqué fabrics, following the manufacturer's instructions for the web. From the traced or photocopied actual-size pattern, cut out one each of pieces A to G. (*Note*: Appliqué piece A, the large blossom, does not have a hole in the middle, but is simply overlapped by flower center B.) For speed, pin pieces on layered, fused fabrics, but pin pieces D and G on fused fabrics that are folded in half, in order to obtain a left and right piece. Cut out the following appliqué pieces: two A from one pink print, two B from another pink print, two C from a third pink print, and four D from a fourth pink print. Cut out eight E leaves from a green print, and one F stem and two G stems from dark green fabric.

3. Fuse the appliqués in place: Remove the paper backing from each appliqué piece and position the appliqué piece on the marked background, pinning to secure. Start with the stems, then add the A and C pieces. Overlap the edges of the C pieces slightly with the D pieces, and center the B circles over the A flowers. Finally, add the leaves. Removing the pins as you go, iron the pieces to fuse them in place.

4. Machine appliqué the edges: Using white thread and a narrow zigzag stitch, go over the edges of each appliqué piece. Refer to the photograph, and if desired, add additional lines of zigzag stitching along the stems.

5. Finishing: Lightly press the block. Referring to the Basic How-To's on page 97, trim the edges of the background fabric ¼" beyond the dash lines, for a 6½" square block with the design centered.

Actual-Size Pattern for the Block

DOGWOOD IN BLOOM
by Margie Lou Hall

This quilt block is made for the breast cancer quilt in loving memory of my friends, Margaret Rasmussen and Billie Cargill who died of breast cancer, and also in gratitude for six months of remission since my October 1999 mastectomy.

Four buds and leaves surround a full blown flower to provide perfect symmetry, like a medallion in miniature. Freezer paper templates and traditional hand appliqué for this design will reward you with a neat and classic look.

What you'll need:
- Fabrics: 7½" square for background (here, ecru with a textural print); small amounts of 2 pink prints, 2 green prints, and a scrap of yellow
- Tracing paper
- Lightbox or sunny window
- Masking tape
- Fabric-marking pencil in color to contrast with background fabric
- Freezer paper
- Fine-tip permanent marker
- Iron and ironing board
- Scissors for paper and for fabric
- Appliqué needle
- Pins
- Fine sewing thread in colors to match appliqué fabrics

What to do:
1. Mark the background: Place a sheet of freezer paper, shiny side down, over the actual-size pattern, and trace the design with a fine-tip permanent marker. Tape the freezer paper pattern on top of a light box or onto a sunny window. Center the over-size square of background fabric wrong side down on top, matching the grain lines of the fabric with the short dash lines around the design (which represent the stitching lines for the block when it is assembled). Keep the fabric from shifting with a bit of tape. Using a fabric-marking pencil, lightly mark the entire appliqué design as well as the dash lines on the fabric. Carefully remove the tape and set aside the marked background fabric and the freezer paper pattern.

2. Make freezer paper templates: Cut out all the appliqué shapes along the marked lines. Position the templates shiny side down on the right sides of the fabrics, leaving ¼" margin all around each piece, and press them in place with a hot, dry iron. Cut out all the pieces, ¼" beyond the edges of the freezer paper. In this way, cut four A buds from pink print, four B stems from light green print, one C flower from pink, one D flower center from yellow, and four E leaves from dark green print.

3. Appliqué: Position the appliqué pieces over the marked background, working in alphabetical order.

Start with buds and overlap them with the stems, add the flower and flower center, and the leaves. Pin to secure, or use small tacking stitches with white thread.

With the freezer paper still in place, make small clips into the seam allowance to within a few threads of the marked line: along inside curves, into V-angles, and across the narrow tips at the ends of the stems and leaves. Refer to the Basic How-To's for Hand Appliqué on page 96. Work on one edge at a time, and turn the edge to the wrong side–unless it is overlapped by another piece. Use thread to match the appliqué fabric. Peel away the freezer paper after the appliqué stitching on each piece is completed.

4. Finishing: Lightly press the completed block. Referring to the Basic How-To's on page 97, trim the edges of the background fabric square to measure 6 1/2" square, with the design centered.

Actual-Size Pattern for the Block

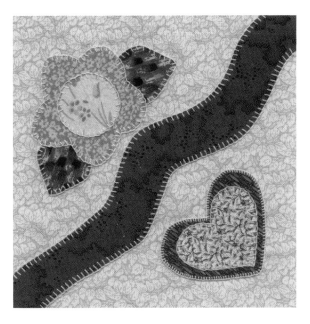

WAVY RIBBON
by Nickie Reynolds

This is my first attempt at quilting. I have chosen a simple design which incorporates the following symbolism: forget-me-not flower—never forget our loved ones; hearts—generations that are affected by breast cancer; pink ribbon path—long and winding trail; hand stitching for the imperfection of life and to show the many steps along the path.

Three sweetly significant motifs are quickly fused in place, then edged with buttonhole-stitching in crisp white pearl cotton.

What you'll need:
- Fabrics: 7½" square for background (here, a beige print); small amounts of 6 prints in different colors
- Tracing paper
- Light box or sunny window
- Masking tape
- Fabric-marking pencil in color to contrast with background fabric
- Iron and ironing board
- Scissors for paper and fabric
- Sewing machine with zigzag stitch and an open toe foot
- White sewing thread

What to do:
1. Mark the background: Photocopy the actual-size pattern or trace it onto a piece of tracing paper. Tape the paper on top of a light box or onto a sunny window. Center the oversize square of background fabric wrong side down on top, matching the grain lines of the fabric with the short dash lines around the design (which represent the stitching lines for the block when it is assembled). Keep the fabric from shifting with a bit of tape. Using a fabric-marking pencil, lightly mark the entire appliqué design as well as the dash lines on the fabric. Carefully remove the tape and set aside the marked background fabric and the pattern.

2. Prepare the appliqués: Apply fusible web to the wrong sides of the appliqué fabrics, following the manufacturer's instructions for the web. From the traced or photocopied actual-size pattern, cut out one each of pieces A to G. For leaves D and E, cut around green area so pieces can be overlapped by flower F. Note that flower center G will sit on top of flower F, just as the inner heart is layered over the outer heart B.

3. Fuse the appliqués in place: Remove the paper backing from each appliqué piece. Working in alphabetical order, position each appliqué on the marked background, pinning to secure. Be sure to insert the edges of the leaves under the flower. Fuse the pieces to the background, removing the pins before you lower the iron onto those areas.

4. Embroider the edges: Using an embroidery needle with one strand of pearl cotton #8 (or three

109

strands of six-strand embroidery floss), work large blanket stitches around all the appliqués except the large heart B. For that appliqué piece, work a smaller version of the same stitch (buttonhole stitch).

5. Finishing: Lightly press the block. Referring to the Basic How-To's on page 97, trim the edges of the background fabric ¼" beyond the dash lines, for a 6½" square block with the design neatly centered.

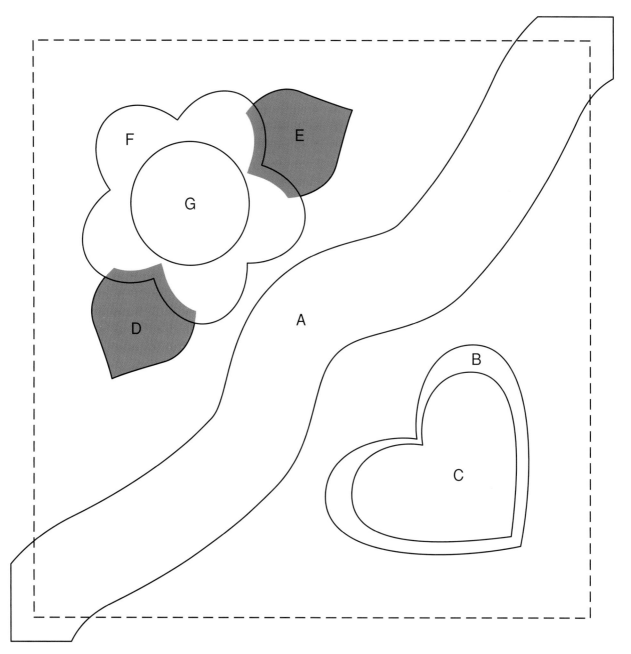

Actual-Size Pattern for the Block

NINE-PATCH HEARTS
by Leslie Deann Brown

The "one out of nine" statistic brought to mind my old favorite, the nine-patch block. The surrounding pink hearts represent the mothers, daughters, sisters, aunts, cousins, nieces, grandmothers, and granddaughters who provide support and comfort in time of need. This is for my aunt Dorothy Jean Garrett. Diagnosed and treated six years ago, she lived cancer-free until this January, when it was discovered her cancer had returned.

A heartfelt variation on the traditional nine-patch block. For ease in assembly, leave yourself with extra-generous margins on your background fabric while you do the appliqué work, and then trim each of the nine patches down to size before you do the piecing.

What you'll need:
- Fabrics: small amounts of red and pink prints (here, the same heart mini prints)
- Small, square quilter's ruler
- Rotary cutter and cutting mat
- Clear or translucent template plastic (optional)
- Iron and ironing board
- Freezer paper
- Fine-tip permanent marker
- Scissors for paper or plastic, and for fabric
- Lead pencil or fabric-marking pencils
- Pins
- Sewing needle
- Sewing thread to match and contrast with the fabrics
- Sewing machine

What to do:
1. Cut out the Nine-Patch backgrounds: Cut out 3" squares from fabrics with the side edges along the fabric grain, one from pink fabric and eight from red fabric. To do this, use a rotary cutter and quilter's ruler and work over a cutting mat. Alternatively, mark and cut out a 3" square from template plastic; place this square template on the wrong side of the fabric, mark around the edges, then use scissors to cut out along the marked line. Note that these patches are oversized, as edges often fray with the handling involved in hand appliqué work. To help with centering the appliqués later, fold each patch horizontally and vertically in half, and press with an iron to crease.

2. Prepare the appliqués: Use a fine-tip permanent marker to trace the outline of the actual-size heart pattern nine times onto freezer paper. Cut out the pieces along the lines, using craft scissors.

Place the freezer paper template, waxy side down, on the right side of the appliqué fabrics, making sure to allow for ¼" seam allowances beyond the freezer paper template edges all around. Using a hot, dry iron, press the freezer paper to adhere it in place. Cut out each appliqué piece a scant ¼" beyond the freezer paper template, for seam allowances. In this way, cut out one heart appliqué from red fabric, and eight hearts from pink fabric. Keep the freezer paper in place until after pieces are appliquéd.

Clip into the seam allowance at the top center of the heart. Thread a sewing needle with contrast color thread. Neatly fold the fabric edges that extend beyond the freezer paper edges to the wrong side, and baste them in place. When the basting is complete, you should see only a sliver of fabric beyond the freezer paper shape. Fold each appliqué in half horizontally and vertically in half, and crease the folds.

3. Appliqué each heart to a patch: Use the horizontal and vertical creases to position a basted appliqué, with the freezer paper still adhered on top, onto the center of a contrast-color patch. Pin to secure. Referring to the Basic How-To's on page 96, and using thread to match the heart, appliqué all around the heart. With the freezer paper left in place it will be easy to stitch through just one thread along the fold of the appliqué.

4. Finish each appliquéd patch: Remove the basting threads, then carefully peel away the freezer paper. Lightly press the unit. Using a quilter's ruler to measure carefully (refer to the Basic How-To's for Trimming on page 97), trim the edges of each patch to measure 2 1/2" square with the heart appliqué centered.

5. Piecing the block: Arrange the pink hearts on red patches around the red heart on a pink patch; refer to the photo on page 111. Stitch the patches together into rows; press the seam allowances toward the center for the top and bottom row, and toward the sides for the center row. Position the top and center rows together. Make a tacking stitch to secure the edges right at the matching seams, and pin at either end of this edge. Stitch, 1/4" from the raw edges. Press the seam allowances away from the center row. Add the bottom row in the same way.

Actual-Size Pattern for Heart Appliqué

CRAZY QUILT BLOCKS
by Leslie Sowden and Sue Walters

Use the directions below as a general guide to the technique of crazy piecing. Raid your stash for fabric scraps, as well as charms, tiny appliqués, embroidery threads, and ribbon to create a unique, personal block.

What you'll need:
- Fabrics: 6 ½" square of thin muslin fabric for foundation, plus scraps of 6 to 12 different fabrics in a pleasing assortment of prints
- Scissors for fabric
- Pins
- Sewing machine
- Thread to match fabrics, or a neutral to blend
- Iron
- Assortment of decorative threads: pearl cotton, six-strand embroidery floss, and/or silk embroidery ribbon
- Embroidery needles

Optional:
- A reference book of embroidery stitches
- Light box
- Fabric-marking pencils
- Small charm
- Seed beads and beading needle
- Small heart-shaped appliqué
- Photo transferred onto fabric

What to do:
1. Starting on a foundation: Lay the thin muslin square on a work surface. This is your foundation, which will be a permanent part of your block and includes ¼" seam allowances all around. Select a fabric you want to place at the center of your crazy patch block; you might wish to consider a photo transfer on fabric, such as the center piece on the block shown at upper right. Use scissors to roughly cut this fabric into a 5-sided shape, so it is larger all around than the #1 piece on either of the actual-size diagrams (page 114 or 116). Pin this piece to the center of the muslin.

The photo on the block is my mother at age 18. Her mother died of breast cancer at age 36. My mother died at age 62.
— Leslie Sowden

This block is in memory of my mom, who was diagnosed with breast cancer at 39 and died when she was 51. She suffered a lot during these 12 years. I was diagnosed in 1999. My prognosis is good. The flowers on the block represent my mom; the buttonhole wheel, the ups and downs of dealing with this; the heart, all of the kind people I have met; 2000 and sun, hopefully the year of the cure!
— Sue Walters

Actual-Size Diagram and Embroidery Patterns

2. Crazy piecing: Next, cut another piece of fabric for piece #2. To closely follow the pattern, cut a chunk at least ¼" larger all around than the piece labeled #2 on the pattern. However, with crazy piecing, you need only ensure that one edge of this piece is longer than the right edge of piece #1. Pin piece #2 right side down on top of piece #1, with the right edges even. Sew a ¼" seam along this right edge. Press open piece #2, using a hot, dry iron.

3. Continuing the piecing: Cut another piece of fabric for piece #3 that measures slightly longer than the top edges of pieces #1 and #2 combined. Pin piece #3 right side down on top of piece #1 and #2 with the top edges even. Sew a ¼" seam along this top edge. Press open piece #3.

Working in rounds like a Log Cabin, add increasingly larger pieces to all sides of the ever-expanding patchwork. After you attach each piece, flip the newly added piece to its right side, and press.

Ensure that the pieces you add around the outside will be ample enough to cover the muslin foundation: First place the pins along the seamline you will be stitching. Fold the new piece over the pins, and check that it will cover the muslin foundation.

Adjust the position as necessary, or cut a new, larger piece of fabric. Pin the piece as before, keeping the pins away from the line of stitching, or removing the pin as the sewing machine needle approaches it. Stitch across the layered fabrics and foundation and press as before. Using this technique will help you keep in mind the ¼" seam allowances all around the block, and avoid adding pieces which would contribute excessive bulk at the edges and corners. When your crazy-pieced block is assembled into your quilt, it will still lay smooth and flat.

4. Avoiding inset seams: Working in the round is the easiest way to do crazy piecing. To simplify the design for the block shown on page 116, the seam between the already-joined 7-5-1-2 pieces and the 8-9-10 pieces has been straightened. To simulate this design quickly and easily, stitch three larger pieces together for a combined 8-9-10. Then, treat this as one piece: Lay it over the completed pieced area, pin, stitch, fold out, and press this final piece into position.

5. Trimming: After the entire muslin square is completely covered, press the entire block with an iron. Using either scissors or a rotary cutter and quilter's ruler, trim away the excess fabric, leaving the piecework even with the edges of the muslin foundation.

6. Embroidery: Refer to the photos for inspiration, and if you are a novice to embroidery, also refer to a book or magazine with embroidery stitch details and information. Strive to use a variety of stitches in assorted colors over the block. Use an embroidery needle with a large enough eye to accommodate the thread, floss, or ribbon you are using. For six-strand floss, separate the strands and use only two or three strands in the needle.

7. Embroidering the seams: Over every seam, use a different linear design, such as blanket stitch, flystitch, straight stitch, cross stitches in a row, or a pattern of zigzags or half-hexagons worked in back-stitches. Embellish these lines of stitching with French knots, single lazy daisy petals, or double cross-stitch stars, as desired.

8. Embroidered motifs: Also use embroidery in more compact designs to fill in empty areas of the crazy-pieced block. To copy any of the designs used in these blocks, trace or photocopy the actual-size pattern, and tape onto a light box or a sunny window. Position the fabric block on top, so the motif shows through where you want it; tape the block to keep it from shifting. Go over the design, using a light pencil or fabric marker. Remove the tape and the block, then cover the markings with embroidery thread, floss, or ribbon. Consider lazy daisy stitches in a cluster or circle, blanket stitches in a circle, chain stitch in rows, or satin stitch to cover a small area. Also consider using pre-embroidered

Actual-Size Diagram and Embroidery Patterns

appliqués, or motifs crocheted with pearl cotton (such as the heart appliqué on piece #7 of the block shown at left). Blindstitch such a motif in place, using thread to match the motif.

9. Silk ribbon embroidery: Use silk or polyester ribbon specified for embroidery, 2mm or 4mm wide. Use an embroidery needle with a long eye that will accommodate the ribbon. Avoid the bulk of a ribbon knot on the back. Instead, begin by leaving a tail of ribbon on the back; pierce it with a subsequent stitch to secure it. To end, bring the ribbon to the back and insert it through a few stitches. As a more secure alternative, use a strand of sewing thread or floss to secure the ribbon ends on the back of your block.

For the pink ribbon motif on piece #8 of the block shown at left, use 4mm silk ribbon, bring it up from the back at point A and down at point D, leaving a loop in the front. Use a strand of sewing thread or floss to secure the ends (A and D), and to tack the ribbon in place at points B and C.

For the ribbon rose on piece #7 of the block shown on page 114, work stem stitches in the round. Begin with a small stitch where you want the center of the flower, then surround it with slightly larger stitches angled to each other and overlapping. Make the leaves with lazy daisy stitches.

10. Beads and Charms: Further embellish embroidery with glass seed beads and small charms or buttons with sew-through holes. Add these after embroidery is completed, and if you anticipate assembling your quilt blocks or quilting by machine, add these trimmings after that, as going over them with the sewing machine may break them.

Use seed beads anywhere you want a dot, as an alternative to a French knot. Use a beading needle and strong sewing thread. For durability, knot and backstitch to secure the thread at the beginning and end, and pass through each bead at least twice. Avoid carrying the thread across the back of the block for more than 1"; end off and start again in the next area.

Attach charms either with tiny stitches in a thread that won't be noticeable, or with decorative embroidery stitches in a contrast color.

11. Finishing: Once the embellished block is completed, avoid pressing, as this would flatten dimensional stitches and could melt beads or polyester ribbon. After the block is assembled into a quilt, use the tip of the iron and a press cloth to smooth out fabric areas that need pressing but take care to avoid embellishments.

HUG & KISS
by Bonnie Monsanto

This block incorporates a hug and a kiss from me to all my sisters past, present and future...The yellow square represents the hope we have that there will be a cure.

If you've always loved the Double Wedding Ring design, here's an opportunity to try a version of it. One ring of wedges, forming a big "O" and signifying a hug, overlaps and encircles a big, pieced X, representing a kiss. Piece the patches, and then simply appliqué them to a background.

What you'll need:
- Fabrics: 7½" square for background (here, a blue solid); small amounts of floral prints: yellow, blue, purple, lavender, and 5 different pink prints
- Clear or translucent template plastic
- Fine-tip permanent marker
- Scissors for paper or plastic, and for fabric
- Fabric-marking pencils
- Sewing needle
- Pins
- Gray sewing thread to blend with all the fabrics
- Sewing machine (optional)
- Iron and ironing board

What to do:
1. Prepare the templates: Using a fine-tip marker on template plastic, trace A, D, and E onto a piece of clear template plastic, using a permanent marker. Use the A template for B and C pieces, which are all the same size square. Cut out the pieces along the lines. For precision and ease, use a craft knife with a rotary ruler to cut along the straight lines; use craft scissors to cut along the curves. Check to make sure templates are accurate by comparing the finished templates with the original patterns.

2. Mark and cut fabrics: Place the template face down on the wrong side of the fabric, positioning one long edge along the fabric grain, and leaving ¼" for seam allowances all around the shape. Trace around, keeping the point of a very sharp or fine fabric marking pencil or pen close to the cut edge of the template. Cut everything out ¼" beyond the marked lines. Along straight template edges, use a rotary cutter and clear quilter's ruler; along the curved edges, eyeball the seam allowance width and use scissors. In this way, cut the following:

From yellow print—one A
From blue print—four B
From lavender print—four C and four E for #1 wedges
From purple print—four D
From each of 5 different pink prints—five E for wedges #2- 6

Also cut out a blue background for the block, 7" square, to be trimmed to size later.

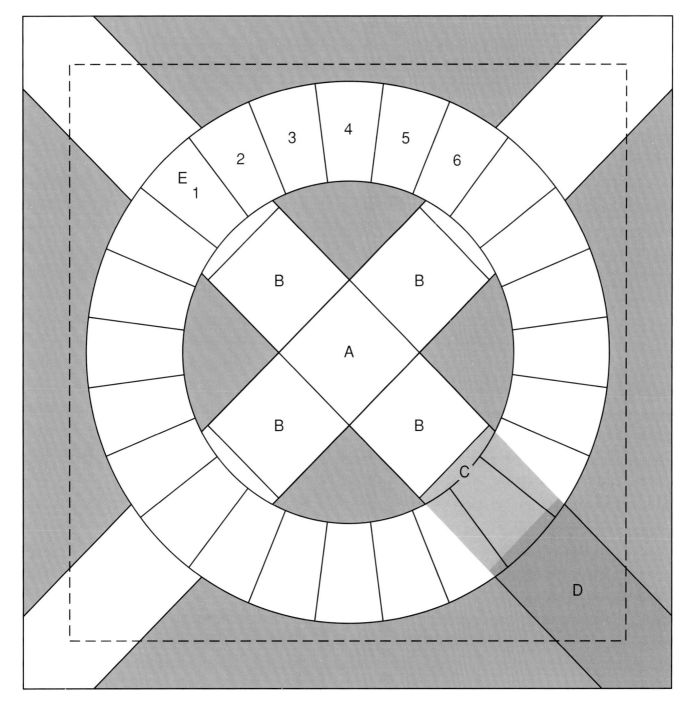

Actual-Size Pattern and Assembly Diagram

3. Piecing: Use gray thread, and hand- or machine-stitch as you prefer. Place pieces together with right sides facing. Pin to secure pieces, but substitute basting stitches or remove the pins as you go; avoid sewing with the machine over them. Unless otherwise indicated, stitch edge to edge across the pieces, along the marked lines and into the seam allowances.

4. Piecing and appliquéing the X: Arrange the A, B, C and D pieces into an X, referring to the colored areas in the lower right quadrant of the actual-size diagram to see how piece C is used in each leg of the X. Stitch four B-C-D units together. Join one of these units to each side of the A piece, but stitch only along the marked line; do not sew into the seam allowances.

Press the long edges of each leg of the X ¼" to the wrong side. Centering the A carefully, pin the completed pieced X to the background. Referring to the Basic How-To's for Appliqué on page 96, appliqué the edges of the X to the background.

5. Piecing and appliquéing the O: Work on top of the background with the pieced and appliquéd X, and refer to the diagram and the photo for placement. Start with a lavender E (1) centered over the C patch in the upper left quadrant of the block. Working clockwise, line up an E wedge from each of the pink prints (2-6) to follow E1, for a total of six E pieces each of a different fabric. Repeat this placement of an E1 over each C patch, and an identically ordered arrangement of E2-6 wedges to follow clockwise, for a total of four arcs. Take the time to assess the arrangement of colors and patterns, and rearrange the wedges to audition other arrangements. If one of the fabrics jumps out too much, or you think more contrast is needed, it's an easy matter to cut more E wedges from different fabrics, and audition other possibilities.

When you are satisfied with the way this ring of E wedges looks over the X and the background, piece the wedges in segments of six, then join the segments together in pairs, and then join the two pairs together to form a complete ring. Press the seam allowances all in the same clockwise direction.

Center the ring over the X, pinning to secure. Appliqué first the inner edge, and then the outer edge. Turn the edges under for about an inch ahead of where you are stitching, and work slowly to obtain a smooth curve. When stitching over a leg of the X, bring your appliqué stitches through C and D pieces but not into the background fabric.

6. Finishing: Press the block. Referring to the Basic How-To's on page 97, trim the edges of the block down so the block measures 6½" square, with the X and O designs centered.

In Canada, daffodils are sold to raise money for breast cancer research. Even in the small scale, the curved piecing in this block is easy, whether you prefer hand or machine stitching. Add a pink ribbon in appliqué.

DAFFODIL MOSAIC
by Joyce Olson

I had just been told my biospy was positive and would need more surgery when the notice of this project arrived, so it seems right that I should participate. My surgery is over and the prognosis is excellent. Early detection is important.

What you'll need:
- Fabrics: small amounts of solid colors: blue, yellow, orange; scrap of pink
- Clear or translucent template plastic
- Fine-tip permanent marker
- Fabric-marking pencils or pens
- Scissors for paper or plastic, and for fabric
- Rotary cutter and cutting mat
- Small clear quilter's ruler
- Sewing needle
- Pins
- Sewing thread in pink and yellow
- Sewing machine (optional)
- Iron and ironing board

What to do:
1. Prepare the templates: Using a fine tip marker on template plastic, trace a 3/4" square, the actual-size patterns for the quarter circle and wedge, and for the mitered framing strip (shown on page 123). For precision and ease, use a craft knife with a rotary ruler to cut along the straight lines; use craft scissors to cut along the curves. Check to make sure templates are accurate by comparing the finished templates with the original patterns.

2. Mark and cut fabrics: Place the template face down on the wrong side of the fabric, positioning the straight edges along the fabric grain (except for the mitered framing strip ends), and leaving 1/2" for seam allowances all around the shape. Trace around, keeping the point of a very sharp or fine fabric marking pencil or pen close to the cut edge of the template. Cut out the mitered framing strip pieces 1/2" beyond marked lines, to allow for inaccuracies in the piecing process. Cut everything else out 1/4" beyond marked lines. Along straight template edges, use a rotary cutter and clear quilter's ruler; along the curved edges, eyeball the seam allowance width and use scissors. In this way, cut the following:

Mitered Framing Strips–4 blue
Squares–8 blue, 7 orange, 5 yellow
Wedges–11 blue, 3 yellow, 2 orange
Quarter-Circles–13 orange, 1 blue, 2 yellow

Also cut out two strips, 1/2" x 2 1/2" from pink fabric, for the ribbon appliqué.

3. Curved Piecing: Refer to the assembly diagram at right to combine a quarter-circle and a wedge into square units as indicated. For each unit, align one of each patch right sides together. With the wedge piece on top, insert a pin at each corner and at the middle. As you stitch around the curve along the marked lines, ease the wedge edge to conform slightly to conform to the quarter-circle's edge. Start and stop at the marked line; do not stitch into the seam allowances.

To join these units with hand-stitching, start and end with a tiny backstitch. In between, make the smallest running stitches you can, to counterbalance the tendency of tiny pieces of fabric to stretch and distort from handling with warm, moist fingers.

To join these units with machine stitching, start and end with a backstitch, and use a smaller than usual stitch–14-16 stitches per inch. Remove the pins before you come to them, and ease the top wedge piece slightly as you round the curve.

Press seam allowances toward the quarter-circle. However, if a darker color fabric shadows through behind the quarter-circle, press seam allowances toward the wedge, or trim seam allowances down to ⅛".

4. More complex units: Modify two of the 11 units that combine one orange quarter-circle and one blue wedge as follows, referring to the diagrams below. For one, add a yellow quarter-circle wedge as shown. For the other, add a yellow wedge as shown.

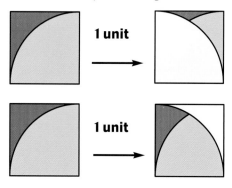

5. Assemble the mosaic: Arrange the squares and square units to match the actual-size diagram on page

124. The black rectangles represent where to insert the ends of the pink strips; turn the edges ⅛" to the wrong side and press, then pin on top of to the adjacent blue square.

Thread the machine with yellow thread. Place adjacent squares and square units together with right sides facing, and stitch them together along the marked seam allowance–but this time, stitch all the way across the edge. In this way, stitch the squares and square units into rows, catching the pink strips in the seams where shown. Press the seam allowances toward the darker fabric, or toward the side with a square rather than a square unit. Pin the rows together, taking care to match the seams, and stitch them together, removing the pins as you go. Press the seam allowances downward.

6. Add the mitered framing strips: Pin the pink strips toward the center of the mosaic to keep them out of the way. Pin a mitered framing strip, centered, along each side of the mosaic. Using blue thread, machine-sew along the marked lines only; do not stitch into the seam allowances. Then place the ends of the adjacent framing strips together with right sides facing, and stitch along their 45-degree ends between the seam allowances only. Press these seams open, and press the seam allowances along the long edges outward toward the edges of the block.

7. Appliqué the pink ribbon: Referring to the photo on page 121, turn each ribbon strip at a 90-degree angle, about ¼" from where it emerges from the seam, so that the ends cross each other. Clip ⅛" into the seam allowances at the turn, and fold these narrow seam allowances to the wrong side; pin or baste to secure. Fold the ends of the ribbon under at a slight angle as shown and pin or baste to secure. Using pink thread and following the basic How-To's for appliqué on page 96, stitch these strips to the background.

8. Finishing: Press the block. Referring to the Basic How-To's on page 97, trim the outer edges of the mitered framing strip so the block measures 6½"

**Actual-Size Patterns for Wedge
and Quarter-Circle**

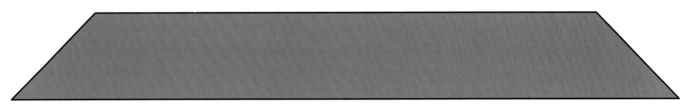

Actual-Size Pattern for Mitered Framing Strip

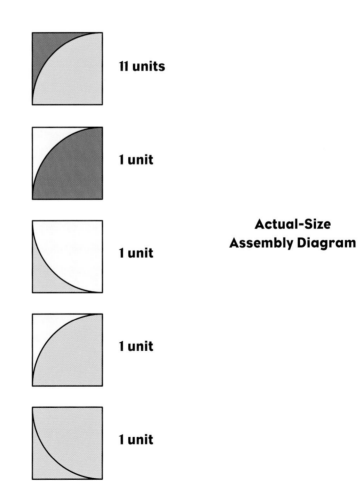

11 units

1 unit

1 unit

**Actual-Size
Assembly Diagram**

1 unit

1 unit

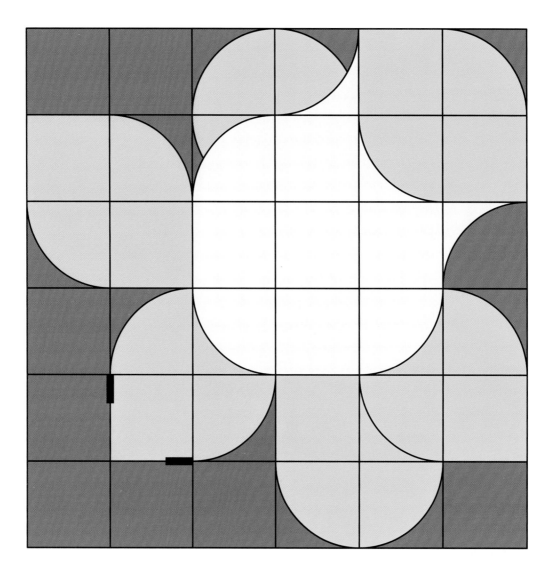

Actual-size Assembly Diagram
(Black Rectangles Indicate Where to Insert Ends of Pink Strips)

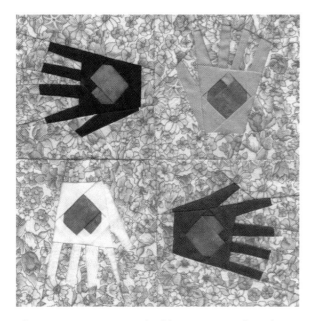

HEART-IN-HAND
by Mary Saint Louis

If you can sew on a marked line, you can foundation piece. This wonderful heart-in-hand block is split into four sections to take advantage of the foundation piecing process. Try making one large single motif on a block before you put *your* heart and hand into the quartet of 3" blocks.

What you'll need:
• Fabrics: For Single-Motif Block, small amounts of fabric for heart, hand, and background; for Four-Patch Block, small amounts of fabric for background, scraps of fabric for hearts, and 4 different fabrics for hands
• Neutral color sewing thread to blend
  with all fabrics
• Thin vellum or tracing paper
• Small, clear ruler
• Fine-tip permanent marker
• Small, sharp scissors
• Glue stick
• Sewing machine
• Pins
• Iron, wooden "iron," or bamboo creaser
• Rotary cutter and small quilter's ruler

What to do:
1. Create the foundation: To start, photocopy the pattern for the Single-Motif Block onto vellum or

copy paper. Alternatively, tape thin vellum or tracing paper over the actual size patterns for the foundation, and trace each of the Sections, I, II, III, and IV, using a small ruler and fine-tip permanent ink pen. Transfer the pattern numbers, too; they indicate the order in which pieces are added. Cut the pieces apart into sections.

2. Position Patch 1: Begin with Section I: the thumb and background. Find or cut a scrap of background fabric about 1¼" x 1¾", and dab the center on the wrong side with glue stick. Place the scrap right side up on the unmarked side of the foundation, centering it over Patch 1. The fabric's edges should extend beyond all four lines of Patch 1 by about ¼ inch to create a stable seam allowance when those seams are sewn. Hold the square for Patch 1 in place, and check the placement by holding the front of the foundation up to a light for a better view.

3. Position Patch 2: For Patch 2, which will be the thumb, choose a fabric for the hand, and cut a strip about 2" x 4". Align it right side down with the raw edge of the center square next to the Patch 2 area. Insert a pin temporarily along the seam line between Patch 1 and 2, then flip the hand fabric over to make sure it covers the space Patch 2 occupies with enough excess for seam allowances. Apply a tiny dab of glue stick to the right side of Patch 2, near the aligned edges of the patches to keep it from shifting when you sew. Flip the fabric back, and remove the silk pin.

4. Stitching: Set your sewing machine to a finer than usual setting–about 16 stitches per inch. With the marked side of the foundation facing up, sew directly on the line that separates Patches 1 and 2, starting and stopping 3 or 4 stitches beyond the line. Remove the block from the machine.

5. Trimming and Pressing: Flip Patch 2 right side up and hold the front side of the foundation up to the light again to check the shadow cast by your new piece. It should extend at least ¹/4" beyond all unsewn lines that surround Patch 2.

Use sharp scissors to trim the seam allowance of Patches 1 and 2 to approximately ¹/4". Finger-press Patch 2 in place or apply gentle pressure using a little wooden iron or a bamboo creaser.

6. Adding Patches: Cut and align a small chunk of the background fabric that will cover the finished area for Patch 3, plus seam allowances all around. Place this Patch 3 right side down over Patch 2, with the adjacent edges even. Pin just to check placement as before, but rely on a dab of glue stick to hold Patch 3 in place for stitching. Flip over to the marked side of the foundation, and sew along the stitching line. Fold the new patch to its right side, and trim as you did before. Add Patch 4 to the other side of Patch 2 in the same way. Finally, place a piece of background fabric for Patch 5 over Patches 4, 2, and 3, and stitch along the seam between these patches. Trim the seam allowances and press the seam allowances as before.

7. Finishing and Assembly: Press the entire Section I, then trim it to the correct size by cutting along the outer solid line, using a rotary cutter and ruler. Complete Sections II and III in the same way. Section IV is a single unit section, and while a paper foundation is not necessary, it will add stability to the assembly process. Also for stability, leave all the

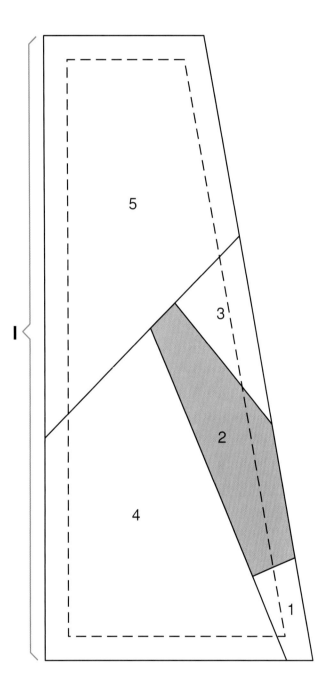

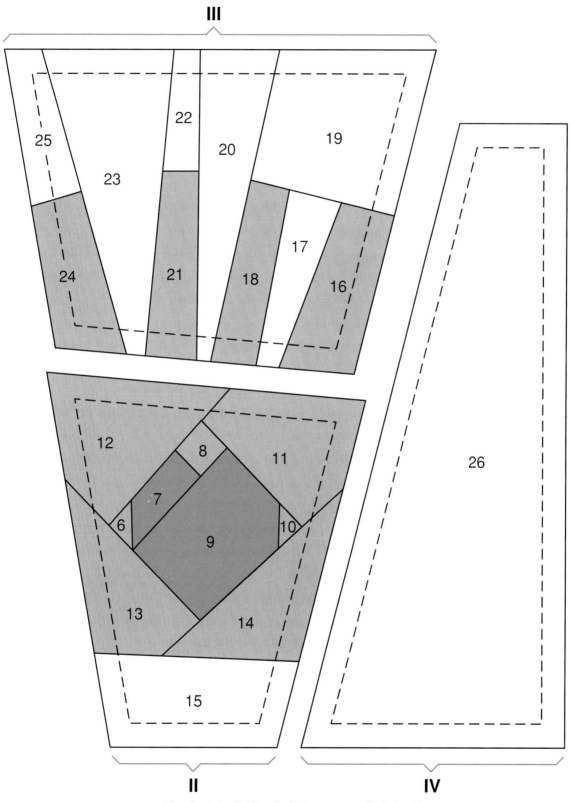

III

25

22

19

20

23

24

21

18

17

16

12

8

11

7

6

10

9

13

14

26

15

II

IV

Single-Motif Block (6" square, finished)

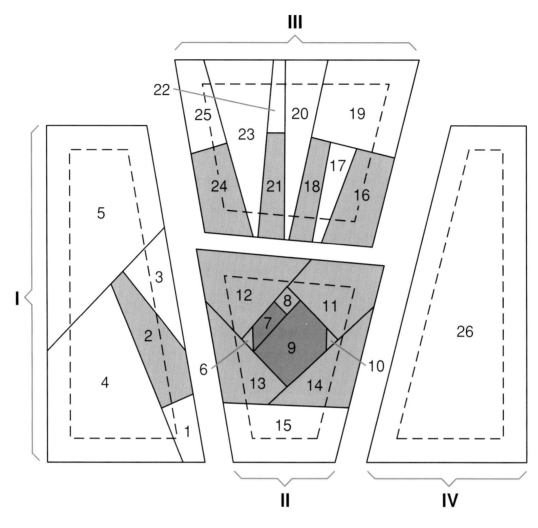

Four-Patch Block (3" square, finished)

foundation paper in place not only until the Sections are assembled but also until the finished block is incorporated into your quilt. At that time, peel away the paper, using a pin to pick off any remaining bits.

Join Sections II and III together, stitching along the dash lines, and press the seam allowances open to avoid bulk. Join Section I to one side of II-III, and IV to the other side. Press the completed block, which should measure 6" square, plus ¼" seam allowances all around.

8. Four-Patch Block: If you would like to hone your foundation piecing skills even further, try mak-

ing the same block in half the size. Refer to the photo on page 125, and photocopy or trace the smaller version of the actual-size pattern four times. Make four of these blocks, using the same fabrics for the background and heart, but four different hand fabrics. Arrange the finished blocks in a two by two set, rotating the hand positions as shown. Pin the blocks together in pairs, with right sides facing and edges even; stitch along the dash lines of the foundation papers. Press the seam allowances open, to reduce bulk. Pin the pairs together in the same way, matching the center seams. Stitch and press as before.

CONTRIBUTORS AND ACKNOWLEDGMENTS

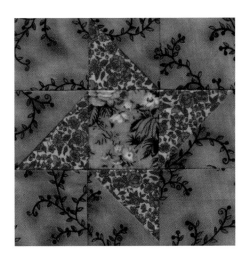

CONTRIBUTORS AND ACKNOWLEDGMENTS

Quilt-Square Contributors

LeeAnn Abdulrahim
Brenda Abplanalp
Barbara Acchino
Audrey A. Ackley
Kathy Adair
Penny Adam
Jane Adams
Oranna C. Adams
Ree Adams
Cloe Adamson
Jean Addy
Betty Ade
Dorothy Adey
Rose Marie Adiska
Maxine Adshead
Selma Agalar
Diana Glynn Ahrendt
Mary Ahrens
Dottie Aitchison
Leigh Akiyama
Carol Aksland
Kathy Alaniz
Betty Albert
Diane Albert
Merlene Albritton
Elizabeth Aleman-Massa
Linda Alexander
Rose E. Alfano
Agnes Algar
Esther Allen
Dorothy Allenson
Sylvia Almack

Elizabeth Althaus
Judi Alvarado
Sandy Amdur
Bobbie Ammann
Mary Jane Ammar
Elsie M. Anderson
Ginny Andersen
Jacquie Anderson
Judith Anderson
Karen B. Anderson
Lauren Anderson

Nadine Anderson
Roseann Anderson
Sarah Anderson
Shirley Anderson
Virginia L. Anderson
Belle Andrade
Mary Andrade
Vicky Andrus
Anne Andrusyszyn
Mary Anttila
Denise Appleyard
Lynn Arce
Angie Archer
Catherine Archer
Maurine Archer
Pamela Argentieri
Martha Armstrong
Maureen Armstrong
Priscilla May Armstrong
Sandy Armstrong
Mariette Arnold
Carol Arny
Carla Arthur
Margaret Asberry
Gladys Asberry
Claire J. Ashe
Jennie Aten
Nancy Aten
Janet Atteberry
Lucille M. Austin
LaTanya S. Autry
Bitsy Avery
Charlotte Avery
Joy Avery
Susan Aylesworth
Michelle F. Aziz
Marisa Azzalina
Veronika Badger
Linda Baile
Aline Kean Bailey
Betsy Bailey
Jane Bailey
Joy Bailey
Nora Bailey
Victoria Bailey
Donna N. Baird
Cindy Bajis
Freda Baker
Lynnis Baker
Mary Baker
Roxann Baker
Sharon Bakke
Bobbi S. Bales
Elaine Ballard
Loni Ballard
Lesa Marie Bame

Shirley Bamett
Martha S. Banks
Helen Bannerman
Kathy Bantle
Ilean Barcus
Catherine Bard
Patricia May Barger
Bunny Barker
Marlene Barkley
Colette Barksdale
Jessica Lynn Barnes
Patricia Barnes
Vonda J. Barnwell
Dolores Barraclough
Marie Barry
Shirley K. Barry
Kathleen Bartels
Karen Barthman
Phyllis Bartholomew
Barbara Bartram
Rosemary Battaglia
Luella G. Bayer
Shirley Baysinger
Helen Bancroft
Pam Beal
Karen Beam
Robin Bean
Nancy Beard
Sallie Beaslin
Irene Bebber
Mary Claire Becker
Teresa Bee
Linda Beecher
Rosemary Beeler
Roxane Beeler
Maria B. Beers
Harriette Beispiel
Eileen Belanger
Wilma Belcher
Betty Bell
Carolyn Bell
Dorothy Bell
Linda Bell
Helen Strub Beller
Daphne Benas
Robin Bennett
Ruby K. Bennett
Tia Marie Bennett
Pam Benson
Sandra Benson
Kathy Benware
Barbara A. Berg
Karina Berger
Ruth Ann Berger
Becky Bergman
June Bergman

Amy Bernhardt
Tarrenz Bersinger
Jeannine W. Bethke
Loretta D. Betz
Rose Marie Collison Beug
Maureen Bickham
Patti Bieber
Patsy Biggs
Dorothy Bilcher
Charla M. Billings
Ida Billings
Della Bingman
Judith Bishop
Janet Bissell

Chris Black
Anne Tucker Blake
Laura Blakely
Stella A. Blanchette
Sally Blohm
Edna Blomquist
Barbara Bloom
Harriet Blose
Erin Bly
Karen Boatman
Reemy Boby
Maryellen Bodell
Myrtle Boggs
Carol K. Bohanan
Gloria Bohannon
Pat Bohn
Regina Boland
Marie Bold
Helena Bolt
Marge Bonenberger
Diane G. Boothe
Robyn L. Borges
Anna Borntreger
Bonnie Bosma
Olivia Boswell
Lois Bosworth
Anne Boucher
Boudrias Family
Karen Bow
Leslie Bowdach
Lana Bowe
Sharon Bowen
Mildred M. Bowers

Irene Bowie
Patricia M. Boxold
Jean Boydstun
Elizabeth Boyer
Liz Ann Boykin
Polly Bracht
Jackie Bradley
Naomi Bradshaw
Joanne Brady
Johnetta Bradshaw
Judy Brach
Peggy Brandon
Elizabeth Brandt
Virginia W. Breen
Sally Bresler
Gladys Brewer
Kippy Brezner
Rosemary A. Bricker
Irene M. Briggs
Janet L. Briggs
Lois Ann Briggs
Linda Brimigion
Diane Brinkley
Barbara Brister
Diana K. Britt
Glenna Brockman
Vicki Brodkin
Lori Brondi
Vicki Brooks
Rosalind Brooks
Marion Broomfield
Audrey Brown
Barbara M. Brown
Betty S. Brown
Carol Brown
Cathy Brown
Charlene Brown
Helen Brown
Karin S. Brown
Kathy Brown
Leslie Deann Brown
Louise Brown
Rosalie Brown
Johanna Brownell
Linda Browning
Linda Broyles
Lee Brumbaugh
Jan Brummond
Diane Brush
Patsy Bruton
A. Lorraine Bryce
Barbara Buchanan
Georgianna Buchanan
Helen Buck
Jane D. Buck
Jena Buckler

Evelyn J. Bugg
Leslie Hope Bulken
Elizabeth A. Buniski
Emily Buras
Wanda Burchett
Rose Anne Burdeny
Barbara T. Burgess
Karin Burghart
Kathleen Burk-Sheldon
Kimberly K. Burk
Patricia Burk
Rachel Burk
Ruthie Burk
Sandra Watson Burk
Beth A. Burke
Joan M. Burke
Tracey Burke
Marlene Bunch
R.M. Burnett

Clara Burney
Elaine R. Burns
Elly Burns-Prestage
Helen M. Burris
Tiffany Burrow
Lorraine Burson
Ellen A. Bush
Gloria Bush
Vicki Bussart
Gladys Butcher
Ruth Butler
Cathy Byrd
Gloria Byrd
Bernice Byrun
Anita Cahoon
Laura D. Calfee
Carole Cameron
Catherine Cameron
Barbara Campbell
Fern G. Campbell
Nancy Campbell
Sally Campbell
Sherry Campbell
Susan J. Cane
Virginia Cannata
Mary J. Cannon
Helen Cantley

Nancy McCarron
  Caponegro
Emelda Cardozo
Irene Carey
Carolyn Carlson
Cathy Carlson
Sherry Carlton
Virginia T. Carmichael
Ellen Carnahan
Connie Carpenter
Catherine Carriveau-
  Isaacson
Sheila Carruth
Mary Cartmill
Vickie Casagrande
Diane M. Caspers
Kay Casperson
Karen Carvel Castleberry
Peggy J. Castor
Andrea Catellier
Beverly Caulier
Elizabeth Cavanaugh
Nancy Cazier
Karen L. Chabot
Dorothy Chaffee
Joyce Champion
Jo Chapel
Sharon Chapman
Yvonne Chapman
Marilyn Chasar
Nancy Chastain

Regina Chester
Chiyoko Childers
Lois Chipper
Louise Chisholm
  East Bridgewater, MA
Louise Chisholm
  Nova Scotia, Canada
Estella Chmielewski
Maurice Choate
Barbara A. Chrisman
Nancy Christenson
Elizabeth Christhilf
Sherry Civil
Martha Clapp
Megan Clapp
Helen Clark

Loretta Clouser
Sue Coates
Cindy T. Cobb
Clarice Cocco
Becky Cohen
Martha Cohen
Debbie Cole
Margo Cole
Frances Coleman
Dianna Loraine Colfer
P. J. Collura
Joanne Comerford
Clara Conant-Castron
Dorothy Connell
Deloris K. Connelly
Eddye B. Conner
Ann Conners
Robin Connors
Jeanette Conrad
Alice Cook
Marlene Cooke
Mary Cooke
Jodonna Cooley
Jay Cooper
Marguerite Cooper
Teresa Cope
Hazel Copenhaver
Barbara A. Coppack
Barbara Corbin
Betty Cornett
Chris Correa
Kathleen Cotter
Grace Cottingham
Joanne Coughi
Dorothy J. Cowan
Esta Cox
Judy Crabb
Johanna Crabtree
Terry L. Crank
Loretta Crawford
Sally Creevy
Barb Creighton
Irene Creighton
Debby Cresanto
Leslie Crisanaz
Patricia L. Crispo
Cherilyn A. Cross
Valerie S. Crook
Nancy Crowley
Cindy Crourse
Diane Cullings
Karen Currier
Anne M. Curti
Marlyn D.
Louise Daenick
June Dahl

Valerie Dale
Michelle Danello
Ruth Daseck
Susan Data-Samtak
Carolyn Davidson
Julie Davidson
Mary Lou Davidson
Paula Davidson
Mary Davies
Augusta Davis
Belinda Davis
Betty J. Davis
Carol Davis
Cindy Davis
Susan C. Davis
Wenda Davis
Joan Dawes
Margaret Dawson
Jean B. Day
Kari Day
Mary Joe Dean
Eileen Debban
Linda Decker
Robin Dederer
Maggie Delaney
Victoria Delgado-Woods
Pamela G. Derry
Jan Deve
Arlene Devine
Cherri Devoe
Shirley Deyoe
Jamie R. DeBates
Schuler DeBruin
Dotty DeCota
Betsey DeFazio
Laura de Graaf
Bridget DeLutis
Glenn D. DeMaria
Lynn DeRoche
Donna DeRossett
Dolly DeSouza
Elizabeth DeSouza
Genie DeVine
Claudia deVries
Doris DeYounge
Marie B. DiGirlande
Gloria Dickey
Mimi Dietrich
Lianne Dillon
Teresa Dipiazza
Norma Dite
Diane Miller Divine
Cary C. Dixon
Hilda Dixon
Lois Dixon
Katherine M. Doan

Betty Dodson
Brenda Dodson
Darlene Doerscher
WillaDene Dohy
Martha K. Dolph
Karen E. Dolton
Shirley Donovan
Susan Donovan
Ruth Doseck
Elizabeth Doty
Rita Doty
Sharon L. Dougherty
Leigh Gaskins Douglas
Louise Doutrich
Elsa Dovidio
Judy Dow
Kathi Downey
Patricia Downey
April J. Downing
Renate Downing
Marianne W. Drake
Susan Drago

Barbara Drayson
Margaret J. Dreshman
Doris Drinnan
Linda C. Driscoll
Evelyn Drumheller
Claire Duff
Judith Duffin
Jacqueline Duggar
Karen Duke
Hazelmay Duncan
Jennifer P. Duncan
Karen Duncan
Kate Duncan
Ruth Duncan
Virginia P. Dunton
Jean Dupree
Dorothy Barry Duprey
Janet Durden
Rosmond Durocher
Madelyn Eads
Phyllis Eaton
Marguerite J. Eberhardt
Lucille Eckerson
Jo Eckert
Barbara L. Edin

Barbara Edwards
Elvia Edwards
Lisa Edwards
Ruchi Edwards
Sue B. Edwards
Debra Eggers
Margaret Eggleston
Cherie Entremont
Lettie Elbrecht
Nancy Kay Elkin
Ruth Ellett
Dianne Ellis
Dottie Ellis
Dolores Ellis
Janice Elsishans
Marcella Emrick
Georgia Emry
Sandie Engle
Pat Englehardt
Ileta English
Maureen English
B. J. Erhardt
Carol L. Erickson
Carlene Erlandson
Gerry Ervey
Margaret W. Esh
Kathy Estep
Grace Evans
JoAnn Evans
Rindy Evans
Barbara Eveleigh
Judi Evinic
Myrna L. Eyre
Jane Fagerstrom
Diane Fahay
Nancy Fahsing
Dianne Fairfield
Nancy Jo Falbe
Beatrice Falcon
Louisa V. Fanning
Nancy L. Farabaugh
Therese Fazekas
Verna Feist
Nina Fennell
Mary Fenwick
Penny Fenwick
Lucy Ference
Mary Lou Ferlatte
Susan Fernandez
Madeleine Fex
Jane Fialcowite
Billye Fietz
Kay Figart
Dorothy Filson
Barbara Findley
Bonnie Fingerhut

Susan C. Finley
Pat Finnerty
Durlyn Finnie
Cathy Firth
Gwyneth Fisher
Karan Fisher

Wanda Fitzpatrick
Ann Flaherty
Dollie Fleming
Jo Fleming
Judy Fleckenstein
Elizabeth Fletcher
Oralia Flores
Frances Flynn
Elaine Foelix
Nettie Folk
Julie Foresman
Andrea Forest
Joyce Forino
Shelly Forster
Frances W. Fortenberry
Sheila Fortin
Julie Ann Fortran
Suzanne Fortunato
Laura M. Foster
Maureen Fosty
Carol Foucault
Julie Fourqurean
Joyce Fowers
Lynn Fowler
Louise P. Fox
Tracie Foxx
Carolyn C. Francis
Claire Francis
Elenore M. Francis
Sharon Francis
Ellen Frank
Wendy Franklin
Mildred Frede
Teresa Fredrickson
Elizabeth B. Freeborg
Lorine Friday
Ora Frierson
Sara Friesen
Christina Fritz
Melanie Fritz
Roberta Fronteras

Majorie Frost
Freda Fry
Rose Fuhr
Patti Fuhrer
Kathleen Fuller
Mary Funkhouser
Grace L. Fujii
Sharon Gabossi
Jackie Browning Gahlinger
Joan Gallagher-Badami
Dawn Galusha
Deb Galvin
Mary Jo Ganote
Brigid Garafola
Janet Peggy Garber
Charlotte Gardner
Judith B. Garfinkel
Sandra Garland
Patricia Garrett
Peggy Garrett
Sherry Garrison
Linda Gassaway
Agnes D. Gates
Charlotte Gates
Lorrie Gauthier
Sonia Gayo
Lucy Gee
Marilyn Geistmann
Marie Gengarelli
Melissa Davis Genson

Elva Jo Gentry
Patti Gentry
Barbara Gerdts
Mollie Gibbons
Paula Gibbons
Chris Gibson
Jama Gibson
Jennifer Gibson
Bonnie A. Giese
Janice Gifford
Mrs. Morris Gile
Mary Jo Gill
Sharon Gillett
Jackie Gilliss
Vera Gillmore
Monah Gilmer
Paula Gilmore

Beverley Gilmour
Ellen Gilson
Mary Ann Ginelli
Gertrude Ginn
Martha Ginn
Carolyn Girvin
Beverly S. Glover
Gertrude L. Goad
Mary Cordelia Godden
Sue P. Godwin
Gwen Goepel
Maria Goetz
Tina Goff
Mary D. Gohr
Beryl Goo
Linda Goodwin
Trish Goldsmith
Alexia L. Gordon, MD
Margie Gorham
Nyla Gorham
Mary Ann Gosch
Kit Gouvin
Betty Gow
Pearl Gower
Ruth Grace
Lindsay Grader
Becky Graham
Jean Graham
Joann Graham
Nancy Grasso
Dorothy Graves
Nadean Graves
Dee Gray
Patricia G. Gray
Barbara Green
Carrie Greenberg
Mary Louise Greenblatt
B. Anne Greene
Dorothy Greer
Elizabeth Greggain
Grace D. Gregory
Charlotte Grelk
Ellen C. Gressman
Sharon E. Griffin
Joyce Griffith
T. H. Griffith
Kristi Asbill Grigsby
Catherine Grimes
Patty Grosch
Muriel A. Grose
Carolee Gross
Kathy Gross
Anita L. Grossman
Diane Grossman
Nancy R. Grossman
Brianna Group

Roberta Grove
Nancy Gruenewald
Maureen Gruerio
Flo A. Grumm
Bethann Grygutis
Judith Guady
Lenore M. Guajardo
Pat Gudowski
Marion Guerrieri
Lena M. Guild
Beth Guilliams
Elizabeth Gundlach
Lynne Gunn
Linda Gurley
Bonnie Gustafson
Carol Gustner
Marjorie Guth
Anna Guthrie

Rebecca Gutierrez
Catherine Guttman
Bonnie Guzman
Edna Gwynn
Rosemary Hackenberger
Lucile Hadley
Dorothy Haines
Mary Lee Hajek
Terry L. Hake
Michelle Hale
Alma Hall
Amanda L. Hall
Connie L. Hall
Eleanor Hall
June Hall
Lola Hall
Lori Hall
Margie Lou Hall
Pat Hall
Cathy Hallatt
Donna Halsey
Jean Halvorson
Ginger Hamilton
Angie Hammonds
Doris Hampton
Sonja Hamric
Dana Hancock
Linda Hancock
Gail C. Hand

Peggy J. Hanley
Nancy L. Hannen
Rita Hannigan
Patty Hanscom
Ida Hansen
Karen Hansen
Beverley Hardie
Karen Hardin
Patricia A. Hare
Annie Hargraves
Donna Harkness
Cheryl Harlan
Carol Harper
Judy Harrington
Sylvia Harrington
Mary Harris
Mary E. Harris-Posther
Penelope Harris
Carol Harrison
Joanne Harrison
Moye S. Harrison
Pauline Harrison
Teresa C. Harry
Melanie Hart
Cheryl Harte
Maxine Hartman
Charlotte Harvey
Donna Harvey
Janine Harvey
Laura Harvey
Margaret R. Harvey
Dona Harwood
Chris Hastings
Dawn Hatch
Barbara Hathaway
Muriel Hathaway
Sharon Hathaway
Lillian Hausmann
Maria Havenhill
Irene Haverland
Deanna Havice
Mary Ann Hayden
Cynthia A. Hazell
Karen Headrick
Betty Heard
Debbie Heard
Gerry Hearn
Irma Heath
Roseann Heath
Erica Hedgpeth
Sherry Hedley
Karen L. Heebner
Christina Heflin
Linda Heier
Therese Heiman
Judy Hein

Marie Helms
Beth Helmstetter
Debbie Helton
Alice Henderson
Gertrude Henderson
Mary Ann Henderson
Patti Henderson
Marcile Henkener
Carolyn Henriksen
Amy Henry
Judy Henry
Ann Herman
Fern Herman
Gloria Hernandez
Pat Richards Herrel
Mary Anne Herring
Leann Herrington
Irene Herrmann
Patricia Hersl
B. J. Herter
Sue Ellen Hewitt
April Heyn
Linda Hiatt
Darcelia Hickey
Dorothy Hicks
Linda Hiehle
Dot Hiers
Verona Highsmith
Marilyn Hile
Debbie Hill
Dianne Hill
Judy Hilton
Nadine Himes
Crystal Hinch
Judy Hines
Susan E. Hinzman
Jan Hise
Dianne Hoagland
Lillian Hobbs
Juanita Hockensmith

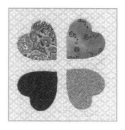

Lu Hocker
Rebecca Hocking
Jeanie Hockins
Susan Hodges
Carrol J. Hoefer
June Hoffman

Veronica Hofman
Connie Hogan
Brook Holbrook
Linda Holbrook
Barbara P. Holding
Christine Hollis
Betty Hollowell
Patsy Holmes
Peggy Holmes
Jenny Holmquist
Doris Holt
Kathy Holtsberry
Donna F. Holzman
Ann Honeywell
Patsy Hood
Marie Hoover
Sue Hopely
Barbara Horacek
Mary Hornicek
Jan Horton
Susan L. Hoshield
Donna Hoskins
Lois Hoskins
Maxine Houchens
Carter Houck
Bobbie Lee Howard
Charlotte Howard
Julia M. Howard
Kaite Howes
Mary Howey
Patricia A. Houston
Barb Hrizdak
Margaret T. Huber
Colleen M. Hubona
Josephine M. Hubona
Ann Huddleston-Souders
Linda (Susie) Hueseman
Cathie Hughes
Joan A. Hughes
Joyce Humphries
Annette Huntoon
Cecilia Huotari
Ann Hurd
Sandy Hurlbut
Laura Hurley
Terry Hutchinson
Wanda Huzel
Maryann C. Hyatt
Trish Hyde
Jean Hyden
Anthony Ibelli
Dorothy Ibelli
Jane Illingworth
Jacquelyn Petersen
    Imbrogno
Pam Ingram

Freeda Ipe
Amy Irwen
Jenny Isaacson
Christine Ischkum
Marie Isenhower
Dianne Jackson
Joan Jackson
Marilyn J. Jackson
Vivian Jackson
Dianne Garon Jacobs
Teri Jacobs
Karen Jacobsen
Carmel Jogae
Lelia James
Vernette James
Dona R. Janefos
Elizabeth Janowitz
Eva Janushuskas
Phyllis L. Jamison-
    Marcus
Sue Jaszcz

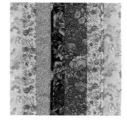

Doris Jenkins
Ilene Jennings
Pauline Jennings
Sylvia Jennings
Anita Jennison
Debbie Jensen
Gaile Jensen
Sandy Jenson
Sheila Jessop
Karie Jewell
Donna J. Joblonicky
Alice Johns
Betty Johnson
Colleen Johnson
Dorothea Johnson
Dorothy Johnson
Enid E. Johnson
Jackie Johnson
Jane Johnson
Jo Johnson
Janet J. Johnson-Foreman
Laurie Johnson
Lonnie Johnson
Mary Alice Johnson
Nita Johnson
Patricia Johnson

Raymond Johnson
Rose Johnson
Sally Johnson
Valerie Johnson
    Shohola, PA
Valerie Johnson
    Watford, Ontario
Vickey Johnson
Dolores Johnston
Kay Johnston
Kristine Johnston
Merle Johnston
Tamara Joramo
Bertha Jones
Donna Jones
Gloria Jones
Irene Jones
Kay Jones
Mary P. Jones
Myrna Jones
Pat Jones
    Rome, NY
Pat Jones
    Southfield, MI
Rita Jones
Ruth S. Jones
Sue Jones
Carol D. Jong
Laureli K. Joosse
Kimberly Joramo-Shipard
Barbara Jordan
Louise Jordan
Helen Joseph
Angela Joyce
Chelsea Joyce
Norma Juern
Mary Julios
Nancy Jupiter
Lucille E. Kader
Cinda Kahl
Carol Rose Kahn
Janice Kalman
Lee Kapus
Nandini Karayan
Judy Karpovich
Ella Mae Kasper
Phyllis A. Kattwinkel
Sandy Keane
Rev. E. Michaella Keener
Marion Keith
Delaine Keller-Little
Myrtle E. Keller
Carol Ann Kellett
Karen Noel Kelley
Marilyn J. Kelley
Maggie Kelling

Kim Kelly
Brinda Kelton
Jackie Kempf
Laura L. Kempfert
Linda L. Kemry
Dannie M. Kennedy
Joan Kennedy
Marie L. Kennedy
Mary Kenney
Carol Kenny
Luella Kephart
Helen Kepner
Marlene Kerber
Thelma Wendel Kerkman
Carol Sue Kern
Emily Sue Kerr
Ann Kester
Jan Kidston
Lisa J. Kiker
Cheryl Killingworth
Lavana J. Kindle
Brenda Kinesrud
Barbara King
Jeana King
Norman J. King
Sylvia Kinney
Barbara Jean Kinsey
Emilie Kimpel
Donna A. Kimura
Annabel L. Kiser
Arleen Kirtland
Yolanda I. Kiss
Melissa Klahre
Gail Kleman
Marlene Kleven
Joan Klier
Deborah Kloss
Mary Margaret Kluge
Lillian Knapp
Janice Knepley
Diana Knight
Lucille Knight
Cyndy Knock
Shannon Knotts
Birgit Knuth
Beth Kodesh
Wakako Kondoh
Mary Kontzelmann
Diane Konzen
Lucy Koonce
Mary A. Kotek
Karen Koterba
Lynda Koziatek
Patricia L. Krall
Donna Kramer
Heather Krane

Linda Kratz-Foote
Karen Ann Krause
Sandy Krebeck
Joyce A. Kreger
Loretta Kremer
Ramona Krile
Maggie Kriz
Pam Krueger
Grace Kuiken
Gail Shaffner Kuntz
Erika Kurasz
Dr. Robin S. Kurtz
Judy Kuykendall
Debbie Kuzemchak
Marion Kyle
Juliana Labbe-Gore
Leslie Lacika
Earlene Lagier
Erin Lale
Janet H. Landreth
Lorraine Landry
Hope Langbaum-Kirsch
Jackie Langelier
Angela Laperle
Deanna Laperle
Mabel Larsen
Linda Larson
Marilyn Larson
Mary Beth Lassiter
Elizabeth Lau
Karen Layher
Velma P. Layman
Kim Layton
Charlene Lazaruk
Amanda Lazorchack
Marilyn League-Glankler
Jacqueline L. Ledford

Catherine (McGreevy)
  Ledgerwood
Kathy Lee
Eleanor-Jean Leighton
Judi Lenchner
Cynthia Lenhard
Susan Lenkowsky-
  Krikorian
Mary Anne Lenyo-Drury
Karen Lenz

Angela Leonard
Lillian Lester
Carol Leuenberger
Barbara J. Levesque
Cathy Lewis
Deborah Lewis
Estelle Lewis
Jone Lewis
Kathy Lewis
Nancy Lewis
Sandy Lewis
Shannon Lewis
Alice D. Ley
Cynthia Likes
Jennie Likes
Virginia Likes
Linda Lindemayer
Pam Lindermuth
Brita Lineburger
Betty Linsley
Marsha Linstad
Catherine Little
Rebecca Littlefield
Hillary Lively
Diane Livezey
Jo Ann Livingston
Debbie Lloyd
Susan Lobravico
Kathleen M. Locke
Lynn Lokken
Beckie Longacre
Barbara Longsworth
Marianne Lopez
Celeste Lorenzen
Sharen Loucks
Anne Lourinia
Gail Love
Beverly Lovett
Joan Low
Zoe R. Lowdoimer
Ann Loyd
Janet Lucas
Sheryl Lucas
Andrea Luchsinger
Ruth Lucius
Karen C. Luckenbach
Victoria B. Lucki
Gayle J. Luczyk
Jean Luddeke
Georgia S. Ludwick
Carleen L. Lund
Jeanette Lund
M. E. (Peggy) Lunde
Phyllis Lundeen
Ina Lundstrom
Jan Lundy-Sharman

Michele Lung
Brenta Lutton
Amalia Lyle
Marlene Lyman
Carol Lynch
Linda MacDonald
Susan MacEachern
Susan MacKenzie
Mildred G. MacLeod
Jill MacPherson
Victoria MacQueen

Ruby A. Mabanta
Nancy Machado
Connie Macias
Claudia Macintosh
Barbara Madsen
Mary Nell Magee
Pat Mahaffey
Joanne Maiden
Jill Majers
Becky Makuch
Miriam Malenius
Tami Mallamo
Diane M. Mandonca
Carmella A. Manges
Martha Manley
Diane M. Manuel
Joan Marchetti
Judy Marino
Karen Marlett
Margaret D. J. Marr
Nancy Mars
Pat Marsh
Sandy Marshall
Constance Lee Marsicano
Betty Martin
Betty C. Martin
Jackie Martin
Katy Martin
Kay Martin
Mary Martin
Stacey B. Martin
Annette Martinez
Elizabeth Martinus
Marjorie Martz
Emily Marziale
Nancy Masannat

Irene Masley
Mary Mason-Rush
Loretta Mateik
Sheeba Mathew
Cindy Matney
Doreen Mattatall
Bonnie Matthews
Icylin Matthu
Laura May
Susan S. May
Beverly Mayo
Cindy Mayan
Dawn Mayers
Jean Ann Mazejy
Shendy McAtee
Carolyn McBride
Jennifer McCann
Margaret McCarraher
Helen McCarthy
Vivian McCarthy
Joan R. McCauley
Elizabeth McClain
Gretchen McClain
Phyllis McClendon
Mrs. Billy McCoy
Melane McCuller
Gean McCullough
Devi McCully
Julia H. McDade
Stella McDonald

Marcella McDowell
Rhonda McDowell
Gail Moffitt McFadden
Carolino McFarland
Nancy McGinnis
Penny McGinnis
Patricia McGraw
June McGuire
Dianne McIntire
LaVerne McIntyre
Claire A. McIvor
Barbara J. McKean
Betty McKelvy
Lisa McKenzie
Roberta McKinney
Cheryl McKnight
Karen McKnight

Marilyn McLain
Tena McMahan
Jean McManus
Jewel McMillan
Lenora McMullen
Jane McNaboe
Marcia McNally
Ruby McNally-May
Donna McNeal
Sheila McNeill
Betty McPeters
Anne McPharlin
Betty M. McQuain
Laurene McRae
Linda McRaven
Pat McSwain
Daisy McTeague
Rose Meese
Deborah Mehlfeder
Vicki Mehrer
Taylor Mei
Louise Meiling
Ann M. Melia
Sue Mellett
Amelia Menking
Pat Mensing
Jo Merecki
Venus Meredith
Erika Merrick
Lori Merrill
Theresa Merritt
Sharlene Meydell
Jodi Meyer
Janet Meyers
Ellen Mierop
Donna J. Milam
Anne Millane
Carol Miller
Jeannette Miller
Jennifer Miller
Kathryn Miller
Kim Miller
MaryAnn Miller
Norma Miller
Olga J. Miller
Pat Miller
Sherry Miller
Beth Mills
Maureen A. Minor
Donna Mitchell
Victoria E. Mitchell
Linda Mitzel
Brandy Mjoen
Sue Mobley
Shirley Moeller
Suzi Moellmann

Grace Moerman
Joanne Mohre
Sandra Mollon
Charlotte Monaghan
Pauline Monroe
Joan D. Mont
Angela Flowers Moore
Dorothy J. Moore
Leslie Moore
Nancy A. Moore
Bonnie Monsanto
Lisa Montagna
Marie Montoya
April Morehouse
Wanda Morgan
Kristina Morris
Ann Morrison
Kay Morrison
Wanita Morrow
Donna Morse
Renie Morse
Ala Mae Acton Morton
Evon Morton
Pat Mosley
Julie Motyleski
Mary Moyer
Gayle Mueller
Helen Mueller
Jeanne Muhl
Debra Mullen
Peggy Muller
Linda Mulpagano
Della Mungazi
Joyce Munson
Ethel M. Murdoch
Elaine M. Murdock
Gay R. Murdock
A. J. Murphey
Margaret Ann Murphy
Mert Murray
Vera Murray
Brenda Murtha
Michelle Murtha
Priscilla Muscolino
Iris Musser
Eleanor Myerly
Sue Myers
Cynthia Myhre
Marianne Myrick
Janet Nash
Verna L. Nash
Vicki Naslund
Claire Neal
Patti C. Neer
Maggie Neilson
Arleen D. Nelson

Elsie Nelson
Kathleen Nelson

Lorna Nelson
Pat Nelson
Sandra E. Nelson
Jean Nemunaitis
Jeanne Neubert
Lil Neuls
Mary Louise Newcomb
Sandra Newcomb
Ruth Newell
Bea Newman
Carol Ann Newman
Anna Marie Nichols
Jan Nicholson
Lois Niebauer
Eileen Nielsen
Hanni Nielsen
Judy Nielsen
Jeanne Nighbor
Alyson Nixon
Arleen A. Nodwell
Peggy Noll
Bessie I. Nora
Doris Nordioh
Ann M. Norman
Anna Norris
Chris Norton
Grace Nothum
Lynne M. Nothum
Jane Novak
Mary Nucilli
Marg Nurse
Betty Nuti
Susan Nycum
Barbara O'Brien
Clara O'Brien
Virginia M. O'Connor
Janet O'Halloran
June D. O'Hara
Mary O'Neal
Bernice O'Rourke
Phyllis Ober
Elizabeth H. Oberlin
Barbara Oberthur
Cheryl Ocean
Anne Odendhal

Patricia Odendhal
Nancy Odom
Helen Oehlke
Kathy Oehlmann
Gail Ogasawara
Koreen Ogg
Diane Ohlsen
Joyce Olson
Lina A. Olsson
Linda Olszewski
Gayle Omansky
Lisa Pieti Opie
Gale Oppenheim
Mickie Orcutt
Cherie Orenstein
Susan Orlikowski
Linda Gail Orozco
Ramona Ortegon
Janice L. Oudt
Jean Overmayer
Linda Overton
Betty Owen
Chalice Owen
Charlotte Owen
Carolyn Owens
Mary Paccia
Shirley Pacia
Ramona Pack
Luella Paddack
Karen Page
Lynn Palangio
Sara W. Palmer
Nancy Palmquist
Muriel Louise Pansarasa
Fran Park
Minnie Parker
Tanna Parker
Roberta Parkhurst
Darlene Parkin
Mary Parr
Jean A. Parrish
Roberta Partridge
Ellen Parks
Carmen Patterson
Judy Patterson
Marian Patterson
Bonnie Paul
Audrey M. Paulsen
Bonnie J. Paulson
Joyce Pavelka
Marie Payne
Sondra Peacock
Rose Pearce
Kathy Pearce-Mueller
Carolyn Peck
Marjory A. Peck

Linda Pedersen
Bobbie S. Peele
Arlene Peet
Beverly Peitz
Nell Pennings

Sherry Percic
Melody Perck
Linda Percy
Tonya Perkins
Gail Perrone
Lauren Perusi
Vera M. Pesce
Barbara Peterson
Carol Petersen
Ivadell Peterson
Jenny Peterson
Mary W. Peterson
Robin Peterson
Doris Petruska
Linda Pettine
Luci Pewsey
Frances E. Pfeifer
Shirley Pfeifer
Teresa Pfieffer
Sarah Philamalee
Audrey Philips
Twalah Phillip
Barbara Phillips
Elmira Phillips
Janet Phillips
Cathy S. Pickett
Leona Pidcock
Marquita Pierce
Patricia L. Pieti
Twila Pilcher
Mary Piltch
Janet Pius
Sandra Player
Bessie Pluid
Diane K. Plunkett
Margaret Pochop
Pat Poe
Marcia Poirier
Jackie Poole
Terri B. Poole
Jimmie Poore
Georgette Pomilia

Alice Joyce Pope
Gwendolyn Pope
Monia Popiel
Beverly Popp
Barbara Porter
Patricia Porter
Doris Porterfield
Jessica Porterfield
Mary Lou Poteat
Cara L. Potin
Nina Potter
Deborah Potts
Carol Poulson
Marilyn Poulton
Ruth Powell
Joan W. Powers
Linda Powley
Diane Powrie
Sharon Prader
Debra Prantl
Lori Preston
Sabrina L. Preston
Mari Pretzer
Susan Prevas
Adva Price
Barbara C. Price
Gloria Price
Meredith Price
Ruth Price
C. J. Johnson Pritchard
Nan Pritchard
Wendy Proulx
Judy Puckett
Ruby Pullens
Phyllis Quam
Diane J. Quayle
Patricia A. Quinlan
Lorna Quiggle
Cynthia K. Quon
Susan Radke
Regina Rael
Carolyn J. Rainey
Katherine Rainey
Lisa Rainey
Diana Rainwater
Victoria Rakowski
Janice Ramage
Ruth Ramsey
Sally Ramsey
Lucy Ranck
Shyamala Rao
Carolyn Rapolas
Lesley Ratcliffe
Mary Ray
Mary Margaret Read
Marcia Redd

Grace Reed
Jo Reece
Jerre Reese
Alesha Reeves
Mary Reeves
Wanda Regula
Linda Reich
Darlene Reid
Jana W. Reilly
Maureen G. Reily
Kathy Reimann
Jane M. Reinhart
Martha Remington
Susan Renker
Carole J. Reusch
P. Rey
Beverly Reynolds
Kathy Reynolds
Nickie Reynolds
Bonnie Rhoby
Shirley Rice
Sherry Rich
Mary Richards
Anne Richardson
Lt. Col. Margaret
 Richardson
Marilyn Richardson
Grace Riggs
Connie Richman
Candy Richmond
Brenda Riffle
Sheila Riffle
Sue Rikala
Mary Elizabeth Riley
Lori Rippey

Angelina S. Rivers
Leslie Rizzo
Frances L. Roark
Ginger Robbins
Patricia Robbins
Christine Roberts
Joanne Roberts
Mary Lou Roberts
Priscilla Roberts
Wilma Roberts
Margaret Robertson
Beverley J. Robinson

Debbie Robinson
Margaret Rose Robinson
Linda Robinson
Sharon L. Robinson
Maggie Robson
Betty G. Rockwell
Martha Margaret
  Rockwood
Doreen Rogers
Natalie Rogers
Diane Rollins
Terry Romito
Karen Romund
Evelyn G. Romzek
Tulia E. Ronda
Cassie Roose
Celene Roose
Marianne Roose
Tammy Roose
Laine Ropson
V. Rosamilia
Mavis Rosbach
Eileen Rose
Reanne Rosenbahm
Janet Rosencrans
Erit Rosenthal
Samantha Roser
Cherylynn Ross
Susan Ross
Geri Rossi
Joanne Rossi
Anne Rothrock
Carolynne Rousch
Jan Rouse
Nanette Rousseau-Smith
Alice Rowe
Sally Boucher Rowe
Sharon C. Rowe
Connie Rowland
Donna Rozich
Karen Elise Rubin
Mary E. Rucker
Mary Jane Rugg
Connie Ruk
Joan Runions
Carole Russell
Deborah Russell
Elizabeth Russell
Lara Russell
Sushi Russell
Thyra Russell
Carol Rutherford
Bobbe Ryback
Barbara Rynders
Margaret Rynn
Janice Sabellico

Barbara Sabol
Kaila Saint Louis
Mary Saint Louis
Sandra L. Sahlstrom
Noella A. Salas
Jeanne Lakatos Salcido
Farida Moiz Salehbhai
Marie-Claude Salembier
Barbara Salisbury
Cindy Salisbury
Elaine Salkil
Shirley Salzbrenner
Karen Sample
NormaJean Samuelsen-
  Brevik
Sandra Sanchez
Sharon Sandberg
Jan Sanderson
April Sandusky
Donna Sanford
Arlene C. Santoro
Beth Sarafian
Alyce Sarsi
Jo Ann Sass
Judy Sauer
Janet Saulsbury

Edna Savage-Moser
Ruth Savasta
Willella Saygrover
Gayle Sayles
Susan M. Scahill-Schichtel
Patricia Scalf
Linda Scallion
Ramona Scarton
Carolyn Schade
Carolynn Schaefer
Mary Jane Schaefer
Martha Schen
Elsie Schenk
Cindy Shilling
Willie Schick
Carol Schippman
Anne Schlosser
Linda Schmaker
Fran Schmidt
Terry Schmidt
Margarete Schmucker

Carol Ann Schneider
Shannon Schooley
Donna Schow
Cleora Schramm
Brook Schroeder
Nancy Schroeder
Tina Schroeder
Jane Schulz
Jini Schultz
Rita Schultz
Audrey Schwartz
Diane Schwarz
Linda Schwind
Jean E. Sciotto
Carilyn Scott
Darlene Scott
LaJuana R. Scruggs
Katie Se
Teresa Sealy
Ann Sears
Christine Seay
Tammy Sedor
Karen Seibel
Lonnie Selby
Judy Semas
Erica Semple
Jane Senyk
Virginia Ann Senyk
Lori Sepanik
Lisa Setzler
Janice C. Sevegny
Dorothy Mae Shaffner
Elaine Shamblen
Nancy Shaulis
Jo Shay
Kae Dee Shay
Klairee Shay
Shelley Shay
Kathleen M. Shea
Annetta Kay Shearer
Noel Shearer
Renee Shediux
Cathy Sheehan
Diane Sheldon
Grace Sheldon
Jessica Sheldon
Mable Shell
Dorlese Shelley
Rhonda Shelly
Heidi Shelton
Lori Shelton
Lynne D. Sherman
Kathy Sherrill
Jenny Shinkfield
Janis Shipley
Dot Shirer

Sharon R. Shirley
Marilyn Shockey
Debbie Shola
Theresa Barry Shostak
Mary Ann Showalter
Josephine Shreeves
Jana M. Shreiner
Esther Shropshire
Barbara Shure
Piper Sickmiller

Mary Sidelinger
Colleen Siegel
Ann Sikes
Rubye Sikes
Karla Silva
Jill Silverstein
Mary Sime
Doris Simmons
Patricia Nemeth Simmons
Gwen Simpson
Kathy Singletary
Barbara W. Singley
Betty W. Sirmon
Sisters—Karen, Judi, Elly,
  and Colleen
Carolyn Sites
Ann Skalski
Grace Skomorowski
Marie Skuffeeda
Dorothy Ash Slack
Louise Slowe
Mary Jane Small
Ashley Smalley
Cathy Smalley
Agnes Miller Smedley
Jennifer Smiljanich
Carla Smith
Dana Smith
Debbie Smith
Dee Smith
Denise Smith
Emma Smith
Mrs. Gary Smith
Helen Smith
Helen M. Smith
Irma Smith

Janie N. Smith
Judy Smith
Kanae Smith
Marlene L. Smith
Meliss Smith
Patricia Smith
Pauline Smith
Roberta R. Smith
Shannon Smith
Susan A. Smith
Virginia M. Smith
Mary Ann Smrz
Jacoba Snellings
Sue Snowden
Ellen Snyder
Karen Snyder

Lisa Snyder
Mary Ellen Solem
Susan Solomon, MD
Charlotte Somerville
Kathi Southfield
Andrea Souza
Leslie Sowden
Polly W. Spahr
Jane Spalding
Janis Spangard
Anne Doumit Sparks
Fay Sparks
Margaret H. Sparks
Winnifred Sparks
Mary Spaulding
Patricia A. Spence
Marilyn Spiegel
Regina Spindler
Cindy Sprague
Kassie Sprague
Annie J. Springer
Cathi Stabler
Joan Stacy
Lisa Stacy
Stephanie Stager
Jane Staiger
Irene Staker
Patricia E. Stancil
Deborah J. Standiford
Helen Lois Stanfill
Katherine Stansell
Joan A. Stebly

Clyda Steed
Elizabeth Steele
Maggie Steele
Mareem Stein
Phyllis Steiner
Carol Steinhauer
Margaret Stemple
Jennie Stephens
Mary Stephenson
Susan Steppler
Ruth Stern
Margaret Stevens
Charlotte Stewart
Connie Stewart
Mimi Stewart
Rita Stewart
Kim Stickney
Elsie Stinson
Jacquie A. Stiver
Mary Nell Stojan
Louise Stokes
Kathy Stoltz
Carol Stone
Linda Muller Stone
Sharon Stonerock
Sharon Storey
Christine Stout
Joann Stout
Lois Strait
Mary Strand
Nancy Strand
Elaine Strange
Mary Streeter
Louise Strickland
Elizabeth Stroup
Jan Struble
Geri Stuart
Helene Studenic
Anita Stumpf
C. J. Sturtevant
Nancy C. Sudduth
Dori Sullivan
Shirley Sullivan
Torry Sullivan
Linda Sunyak
Katherine Surrey
Debbie Sutter
Libby Swad
Mildred Swaney
Paula Sweth
Margie Swoyer
Mary Jane Swartz
Loretta Swayzer
Ariel Taivalkoski
Betty Rae Taivalkoski
Nancy Faye Talley
Tammy

Corinne Tancock
Dianne Tang
Carol Taranto
Sara Tarhox
Miriam Tarlton
Catherine Tate
Eleanor Taub
Anne M. Taylor
Audra C. Taylor
Debbie Taylor
Dorothy Taylor
Joan Taylor
Karen Jean Taylor
Marie Taylor
Regina Taylor
Roberta Taylor
Heather G. Telman
Nancy TenHulzen
Janet TerBest
Carol Terriah
Dorothea Thackrey
Charlotte Theriault
Caryl-Beth Thomas
Charlotte F. Thomas
Connie R. Thomas
Elaine R. Thomas
Gail D. Thomas
Mary Beth Thomas
Pam Thomas
Peggy Thomas
Barbara Thompson
Beth Thompson
Faye Thompson
Melenda Thompson
Susan Thompson
Carolyn Thornton
Linda Throckmorton
Barbara Thurston
Edith Tiedt
Diane Tietjen
Joann Tighe

Barbara Timby
Erma Tnelin
Carol Todd
Dolores Tolley
Sherie Tomek
Linda Tong
Nancy Torres

Karen A. Toscano
Providence Tota
Mary Lou Townley
Debra Gross Tozev
Marie Trider
Ursula Trimble
Jeanne Tron
Paula Trumble
Carol Tubman
Joy L. Tucker
Shannon Tucker
Nancy Tuer
Lorena Turner
Mary A. Tuttle
Barbara Tuzio
Louise Twyman
Clara Tyree
Mildred Ulrich
Sharon Ulrich
Helen Umstead
Wanda Uncapher
Kathryn Sue Updike
Judith Utphall
Madeline Utter
Lorraine Rose Vaca
Melanie Vaden
Beth Valvo
Sue Vann
Jane VanBoxtel
Pat VanBrandenburg
Pam Van Curen
Billie Vanderer
Evalyn VanDervort
Andrea VanOutryve
Janice VanSomeren-
   Thomas
Patti Van Vuren
Karen VanZytveld
Cherille VanWinkle
Barbara Vaughn
Janet Vaughn
Verla Veasey
Sonya Velazquez
Rosalea Vencil
Mabel Verigin
Linda VerMeer
Megan E. Vichich
Betty Voreis
Donna Voreis
Diane M. Vos
Dolores Vrooman
Lillian Wade
Rosemary Wagner
Carol Wahl
Magda Waldberg
Sharon Wale
Chrissy Ahrendt Walker

Cyndi Walker
Rieta Walker
Alma Wallace
Alice Wallenberg
Sally Walrath
Debbie Walsh
Donna Walsh
Shonny Walter
Leanne Walters
Sue Walters
Lorane Walton
Elizabeth Waltrip
Virginia Walworth

Shirley Ward
Linda Ware
Sharma-Lynn Warford
Mavis Warland
Elizabeth Warner
Ruth Warren
Doris L. Warriner
Charron Warrington
Lisa Warshal
Rhonda Washburn
Marianne Watada
Denise Waterfield
Karen Watkins-Brown
Kristina Watson
Mary Jean Watson
Pat Watson
Lou Ann Watt
Sarah Watters
Carolyn Watts
Constance Waxter
Jeannine Wayman
Bonnie Weaver
Eileen Weber
Pam Weber
Frances Wedgewood
Mary Weglarz
Joan Wegman
Dorothy Weimann
Rita Weiss
Ferne Weissman
Deborah Welch
Kathy Wells
Kimberly Wester
Margaret Weston
Anita Whalen

Lucille Whatly
Susan Wheatley
Cynthia Wheelehan
Cynthia Wheeler
Anna White
Barbara White
Linda White
Mary Lou White
Muriel White
Valerie White
Christine Whited
Trish Whiteside
Jeanne Whittle
Trudy Wick
Sherry Wiedow
Lane Wight
Colleen Wilber
Loraine Wilburn
Joyce Wilcox
Juanita J. Wilcox
Joan Wilcynski
Mary Wildsmith
Shirley Wiles
Joyce Wilke
Joan Wilken
Wanda Wilkes
Laurie Wilkey
Jody Wilkinson
Cindy Williams
Eileen Williams
Evelyn L. Williams
Lynn Williams
Cheryl Willis
Ruby Williams
Sarah Williams
   Fort Worth, TX
Sarah Williams
   Cincinnati, OH
Ila Willis
Barbara Willoughby
Doralee Wilson
Doris Wilson
Katie Wilson
Marcie Wilson
Marty Wilson
Sally R. Wilson
Willa Wilson
Kris Winkler
Sally Winn
Barbara Winslow
Beverly Winther
Carol Ann Winther
Jonne Winter
Ada L. Wirbel
Fay Judith Stevens Wirth
Carole Wishart-Anderson
Brenda Witters

Charlotte Witwer
Lorraine J. Wojcik
Noreen Wojcik
Kay Wolff
Lyn Woodley
Judy Wood
Cindy Woodrow
Maybelle Woods
Wilma Woods
Julia H. (Kay) Woodson
Margo Woolard
Amy Worden
Midge Worden
Cynthia Worl
Linda Wright
Irene Wylie
Evelyn Wyse
Mary Yager
Cindy Yamamoto
Linda Yates
Suzanne B. Yauch
Ruth Ann Yax
Ketha Yencer
Kathy Yeo
Daisy Yerian
Linda J. Young
Susan Young
Mary Zachary-Lang
Evangeline Zarras
Sue Zeller
Christa F. Zemlin
Barbara Zercher
Diane Zettler
Andrea Zimmerman
Shirley A. Zimmerman
Millie Zoellner
Kathy Zook
Nancy Zrinszki

Quilt Groups Who Contributed Blocks

AFRO-AMERICAN QUILTERS GUILD
Los Angeles, CA

BALDWIN PARK SATURDAY MORNING
CLASS-Y QUILTERS
Baldwin Park, CA

BOTHWELL'S CORNER 4H
Owen Sound, Ontario

BRADFORD VILLAGE QUILTERS
Santee, SC

CALHOUN COUNTY QUILT GUILD
Victoria, TX; Seadrift, TX; Port
Lavaca, TX; Kiowa, OK

CALICO CATS QUILT GROUP
Danbury, CT; Sherman, CT
Agawam, MA; New Fairfield, CT

CALICO CUT-UPS

CLINTON COUNTY EXTENSION
HOMEMAKERS MAUPIN CLUB
Byrdstown, TN; Albany, KY

THE COPING CLUB
Brooklyn, NY

COUNTY CONNECTIONS CLUB
Mark Center, OH; Ney, OH

COURTHAUS QUILTERS
Monroe, WI

DELAWARE PIECEMAKERS
Powell, OH

DORCAS SEWING MINISTRY
Flagstaff, AZ

ELLINGTON QUILT CLUB
Tolland, CT

ESSEX COUNTY QUILTERS
Fairfield, NJ

FAIRVIEW QUILT CLUB
Fairview, MO

FIRST BAPTIST PIECEMAKERS
Gilmer, TX

FOOTHILLS QUILTERS GUILD
Sieverville, TN; Alcoa, TN
Maryville, TN; Knoxville, TN

FOLEY WOMEN OF TODAY

FT. ST. JOHN QUILTER'S GUILD
British Columbia, Canada

GOLDEN NEEDLES QUILT GUILD
Conroe, TX; Spring, TX

GRAND STRAND QUILTERS

GRAPEVINE-COLLEYVILLE
NEIGHBORHOOD AMERICAN
SEWING GUILD

HARRIET TUBMAN RESIDENTIAL CENTER
Auburn, NY

IRONDEQUOIT QUILT CLUB
Rochester, NY

ISLAND THREADS
Pawley's Island, SC

JUNIATA VALLEY QUILTER'S GUILD
Belleville, PA

KLAMATH INN QUILTERS
Klamath, CA

KOOTENAI VALLEY QUILTERS GUILD
Libby, MT

KOTTAGE QUILTERS
Snowflake, AZ

LADIES OF THE LAKE QUILT GUILD
Polk City, FL; Lakeland, FL

LAKE MARION PIECEMAKERS

LAKE POWELL QUILTERS
Page, AZ

LAUREN'S HAPPY QUILTERS
Dublin, GA

LIGHTHOUSE QUILT GUILD
Crescent City, CA

LOG CABIN QUILTERS GUILD
Elkins, WV

MANTECA QUILTERS
Stockton, CA; Tracy, CA

MILFORD VALLEY QUILTERS
Milford, PA

MILTON KWAZI KWILTERS
Oak Ridge, NJ

MIRAMICHI QUILT GUILD

MOUNT AIRY BOBINETTES
Damascus, MD

NEEDLEMANIA CLUB
Needles, CA

NEEDLES & THREADS QUILTERS GUILD
Chicago, IL

THE NEEDLES RULES SOCIETY
Detroit, MI

NINE NEEDLES SEWING CLUB

NORTH EAST IOWA QUILTERS
Decorah, IA

OAK RUN QUILTERS
Ocala, FL

OHIO LAUREATE GAMMA LAMBDA

OHIO STAR QUILT GUILD

PIECEMAKERS FIRST BAPTIST CHURCH
QUILTING GROUP
Gilmer, TX

PINE TREE QUILTERS
Madison, FL

PLEASANT RIDGE COMMUNITY CENTER
Cincinnati, OH

THE QUILT CONNECTION
Chicago, IL

QUILTERS FOR RESTORATIVE JUSTICE
Shakopee, MN

RED & WHITE QUILTERS
Rome, NY

REFUGIO COUNTY QUILT GUILD

RHEINLAND PFALZ DISTRICT QUILTERS
Germany

SACHEM QUILTERS
S. Weymouth, MA; Halifax, MA

SAMARITAN BETHANY HEIGHTS
RESIDENT QUILTING BEE

ST. CLAIR COUNTY QUILT GUILD
Lowry City, MO; Appleton City, MO;
Osceola, MO

THE SEW & SEWS
Tsauwassen, BC, Canada

SIMI VALLEY ADULT SCHOOL
Simi Valley, CA

STITCH & BITCH
N. Branford, CT

STRASBURG COUNTRY QUILTERS
Strasburg, CO

TENDER LOVIN' QUILTERS
Troy, MT

THOUSAND ISLAND'S QUILTER'S GUILD
Mallorytown, Ontario

WESTERN WAYNE COUNTY
QUILT GUILD
Ypsilanti, MI; Belleville, MI

WHISPERING CRAFTERS
DeLand, FL

Girl Scout/Brownie Troops

Brownie Troop
Perrysville, IN

Brownie Troop 70
Damascus, MD

Brownie Troop 125
Mohawk, MI

Girl Scout Troop
Perrysville, IN

Girl Scout Troop 188
Boyds, MD; Clarksburg, MD

Girl Scout Troop 288
Central Lake, MI

Volunteers At Our Quilting Marathon Weekend, July 9-11, 2000

B. J. Berti, CRAFTER'S CHOICE
Sally Davis, THE QUILT CONNECTION
Lois Griffin, THE QUILT CONNECTION

Diana Ahrendt
Ellen Bardolf
Linda Basilio
Alicia Bell
Carol Benner
Jean Biddick
Bettina Bierly
Linda Bittrich
Elaine Blumgart
Janis Blumgart
Phyllis Borzotta
Kathy Bower
Eileen Boylan
Connie Buchanan
Lucy Bureau
Ellen M. Burke
Carolyn Carmichael
Caterina Caron
Rachel Cochran
Phyllis M. Conrad
Dot Davis
Rita Erickson
Eileen Eyerman
Mary Ellen Gallico
Alison Gardner
Neelima Giokhale
Carol Grant
Sandy Greenfield
Esther Greenfield
Maggie Griffin
Janice Hairston
Natalie S. Hart
Magi Heffler
Debbie Hennessey
Esther Hirschfield
Kathie Holland
Verdi Johnson
Carol Kadlic
Dot Kish
Ellie Leght
Sandy Mackay
Jane Mahan
Delano May
Dale Mazzei
Liz Mershon
Sonya Morgan
Florence Murphy
Kathleen Nitzsche
Deanna Peterson
Melda Pike
Vincenza Pompa
Linda S. Pote
Dolores Reiman

Betty Remurs
Marjorie Rice
Stacey Salisbury
Beth Sanders
Barbara Schaffer
Eileen E. Schmidt
Tina Schmidt
Eric W. Schmidt
Dorothy Scull
Monika Snisky
Patricia St. Pierre
Colleen Steiner
Liz Topper
Marisa Toroker
Irene Veblaitis
Betsy Vinegrad
Laura Wagner
Ellen Walsh-Sobel
Betty Woerner

Volunteers Who Assembled and Quilted the Quilts

Linda Basilio
Cindy Boyde
Gail Broadwater
Linda Causee
Kris Carlson
Barbara Epperson
Sue Ewing
Sandy Klop
Cindy Kurpiewski
Helene Kusnitz
Sherline Lockhart
Rhoda Lonergan
Vicki Nelson
Linda Roberts
Marinda Stewart
Linda Walsh
Valerie Zeman

Donors

- Janome–for the use of sewing machines
- P&B Textiles–Mr. Irwin Bear
- Hobbs Bonded Fibers– Mr. H. D. Wilbanks

Special Thanks

- Jane Hamada at Martingale & Company
- Trish Katz at C&T Publishing
- Rita Weiss at the American School of Needlework